MORE HUMOROUS HUNTING CAMP STORIES
(A U.P. SEQUEL, VOL #3)

By the U.P. Rabbit
Robert R. Hruska

More Humorous Hunting Camp Stories
(A U.P. Sequel, Vol. #3)

First Edition: 2001
Copyright © 2001
ISBN # 0-9668265-2-3

Published by
McNaughton & Gunn, Inc.
960 Woodlawn Drive
Saline, Michigan 48176

All inquires should be addressed to:
Robert R. Hruska, Author
140 S. Birch Avenue
Gillett, Wisconsin 54124
Telephone: (920) 855-2996

Illustrations by:
Brian Fretig, Teacher, Sportsman, and Friend

Dedication

To my wife, Barbara, who has helped warm up the camp on many a cold nights.

Table of Contents

Chapter 1

The Time "Joe WEASEL" Hired Out As A Hunting Guide

All of the locals knew Joe Weasel well. I think his real name was Joe Sibilski. Ever since I knew him, he was always called Joe Weasel.

He dressed like a sportsman, looked like a sportsman and told stories about his successful hunting and fishing trips so convincingly that if we didn't know him better, you'd believe him.

He normally got a lot of free drinks of "Polish Holy Water" as Joe called it, from big city hunters. They usually visited the local bars at deer season, listened where the hunting action was and the next day, they'd try to find a place to hunt over there.

Joe Weasel was on to these guys. He always talked loud anyway but would talk louder when he'd see the new-clothes, clean looking, tourist-type hunters come into the bar. Joe would have made a good "barker" at a carnival. He knew the kind of "trigger words" these deerless hunters were listening for. He'd talk loudly about the 10 pointer that he couldn't quite get in his sights yesterday because a chick-a-dee landed on his gun barrel.

Then, how he shot a 6 pointer last Monday for the "poor widow lady" who lived a mile down the road. He said, "The bigger bucks are sure plentiful this year." The city hunters (Joe always called them Chicago hunters) started to smile and move closer to Joe. He would later tell us, "I put out the bait for them. Now, all I had to do was jiggle it a little and I normally could catch a few free drinks from them."

One said, "Hey, can I buy you a drink? Sounds like you really know where the deer are. We're kind of beginners at this. Can you tell us some more?" Joe later laughed and said, "I didn't even have to reel them in. They jumped right into the boat."

"Sure, sure," Joe said. "Always nice to meet new friends. I'm drinking Coors." (Joe would always move up a notch when a stranger was buying.) They later said, "Joe, we have to go back home in two days and we're getting desperate. We hunted for over a week and saw only five deer in a field near a house. We didn't shoot as we didn't want to hit the house." "You did the right thing, boys." Joe said. "Never shoot no houses." (Joe Weasel had his own house near there.)

Then they said, "Joe, (They were trying to get personal with him, fast) we are thinking of hiring some local here to take us to a good deer hunting area so we could shoot a buck or two. You know, to take home. Would you consider guiding us tomorrow?"

Joe couldn't believe it. Free drinks and now they wanted to give him still more. He looked hard at the tall hunter, rubbed his chin with his hand, and then said, "I can't help but admire that nice, insulated hunting vest that you have.

Woolrich you say? You sure are a good judge of good hunting clothes." The hunter smiled at the nice compliment. I figured, Oh Oh, that guy better not take off that vest and go to the toilet. That vest and Joe will be long gone when he comes back.

Joe told them, "I'd be glad to help a couple of nice guys like you. The only thing, the County Forester, and some loggers are cutting an 80 to the west of here. He normally pays me something to watch out for his equipment."

The County Forester probably told Joe, "I'll give you $5.00, Joe, to watch these extra 5 axes, 2 chain saws, and 2 cans of gas. I know you are a good 'watcher', Joe, so I'm sure when we come out of the woods, none of it will be missing."

He figured that the $5.00 was cheap payment to have Joe not steal their equipment and no one else in the area had the nerve to tangle with the County Forester.

After another "Polish Holy Water," as Joe called it, he said, "Fellas, I feel bad that you came so far and didn't get a deer. I know a place where the bucks are almost tame. If you fellas can shoot straight and don't mind shooting a standing or walking deer, I'll help you out." Now, these hunters were REALLY excited. They were as excited as going out on the first day. Joe continued, "Just don't say nothing about this to the other locals in this bar. They don't like it when one of us helps strangers like you out. I don't quite understand it. But that's the way it is."

The rest of the "good ole boys" in there were all listening to Joe "put the final touches" onto these "Chicago" hunters. Their shoulders were jumping up and down as they were smiling and trying to suppress some good belly laughs. Two of the locals had tears running down their cheeks as they tried to look real serious and not interfere with Joe Weasel's deal. After all, the "Weasel" had a reputation to uphold. He wasn't called Joe Weasel for nothing...

The locals could hardly wait for Joe to tell them the end of this story when it climaxed. Joe said to the hunters, "Boys, I'll be real up-front with you. You guys are desperate to get a nice buck.. I know where they are and I think I can help you. It will cost you a few bucks, though, only for expenses though, mind you. We'll also have to drive quite late tonight farther north. Waaaaaaay farther north. Remember, its pretty well shot out around here now." The hunters all nodded in agreement. "That means, we'll have to stay in a motel tonight up there. You have such a short time to hunt, we won't cook meals. I'd bring my cook with, it wouldn't cost you anything extra for my cook except we don't have a lot of time for that. We'll have to "eat out" so we can hunt more."

The shoulders on the "locals" started to jump up and down again. Most of them had to look away from the hunters. Their laughter was getting uncontrollable. Joe never got around to getting married yet and never had a cook. "About a hundred bucks from each of you should cover expenses," continued Joe, " I won't charge you for my services, No Sir!!! You have been real friendly, don't mind buying me drinks, now, only a motel room and a few meals. I only hope I can deliver a nice buck for each

4

of you in this private spot that I know." "If you see fit to give me something after the trip," Joe continued on sincerely, "well, that will be up to you. I'll not expect or charge you anything.' "We need more friendly strangers the likes of you around here, yes sir!"

Joe told us that, two hours later, they were on their way. A little more "social drinking" while Joe filled them in on how to "sneak-hunt" and to follow him quietly through the woods. Talking was the worst thing they could do where he was taking them hunting. Joe said, "Boys, this is the last of the great places to hunt this late in the season where I can show you deer. It only stands to reason, the quieter that we all are the better. You don't want to goof up this good chance."

They were REALLY excited then. Joe looked satisfied. They looked like they would do anything that he told them. After a late meal of "prime rib" which Joe told them was the meal of choice of deer hunters, they checked into a AAA motel. Joe told them that he picked this place special. He told them that the other local motels may be "gamey" so they didn't take a chance. Besides, Joe wanted a nice bath with the free shampoos and bath oils that this better motel provided.

"Let me explain one thing," Joe said. "I'm going to insist on having my own room. You know, I can hear a deer breathe at least 100 yards away. If I have another person in my room, it could make it hard for me to sleep and I wouldn't be fresh and ready to deliver for you fine hunters tomorrow."

These "Chicago" hunters were gullible but they were not stupid. By now, they were starting to size up the

5

expenses Joe Weasel was costing them. They were just hopeful that he was the "Daniel Boone" that he seemed to be and they didn't want to believe that the stories he told them of the coming hunt weren't true.

The next day, at daybreak, the hunters awoke, dressed, and went looking for Joe. All they could hear was heavy snoring from his room. They pounded on the door. The snoring noise stopped quickly and Joe came to the door pulling up his suspenders. "What, what, what's all the noise about?"

They said, impatiently, "Its daybreak, we should be out hunting!" Joe smiled. "Don't worry boys. Where I'm taking you, no one else hunts there. It's a secret place. Give those deer a chance to walk around and relax. We'll get them, even later into the day.' They then felt a little better and relaxed.

After a double order of pancakes, eggs, and five cups of coffee, Joe Weasel said, "Now we're ready boys, now we're ready. Just be sure, when I show you deer, don't miss the shots." These guys were now, beside themselves with excitement. A real native, showing them the "mother lode" of places to get a nice buck.

They all got into the car. Joe was in the front seat on the passenger's side giving directions. "We have to drive north again. We could have driven farther last night, but then we'd have missed that nice motel." They ignored that, feeling, they were finally on their way.

One of them saw a tall, fire tower off at a distance. They never saw one before so they asked Joe. "What's that?" Without hesitation, Joe said, "That a Polish Deer Blind."

They looked dumbfounded. One finally said, 'That's a hell of a long ways up there." Joe said, "Yeah, …. the Polish people up here got real good eyes.' The shorter hunter said, "Wait until we tell them about THAT back home." Joe just looked out the window, blankly.

"Its about five more miles and three more side roads to go. When you get out of the car, remember, shut the doors quietly, load up, and be ready to shoot when I point out a nice buck for you. And, above all, don't talk. Deer scare real easy if they hear someone talking."

These boys were now, REALLY excited! Joe seemed so confident that they were going to see deer that it HAD to be true! Besides, he couldn't be buffaloing them because he had to ride back with them. These "Chicago" guys felt that they knew how to fix someone's wagon if they were taken advantage of. This HAD to be true!!

They were forgetting the extra costs that Joe called "normal expenses" and were ready to go. Joe got out the car, stretched, and motioned everyone to be quiet. "Remember all the directions that I gave you." Joe felt that he'd taken them for a walk through some real thick cedars so they felt that they got their money's worth. After a half hour of this, the hunters said, "Joe, are you sure you know where you are going?" Joe looked blank, stared straight ahead and said, "I do believe that we are lost."

Now, they were really getting suspicious. Even Chicago guys can sense a con artist. Joe quickly recovered though and said, "Don't worry, I can find my way out of any woods, even in the dark." They again, relaxed a bit …… then so did Joe Weasel …... He said, "Lets see ….. the

7

sun always comes up east, don't it?" They moved their fingers closer to their gun's safety.

Joe gave a quick smile and said, "Just kidding guys, just kidding. Follow me and don't talk or even think. If you talk, I can't guarantee a nice buck for you." Joe found a way to keep them from plotting to "do him in."

Then, just like you see a professional guide hold up his finger to his mouth, crouch down, walk like a duck, slowly, ever so slowly, Joe motioned for them to do the same. He looked back at them squatting and walking like a duck following in a line behind him. Joe smiled and just shook his head. These "Chicago' hunters would do anything he asked of them. Joe was starting to think ahead for the next year.

He motioned them together in a tight circle. "I've got to give you some last minute instructions. Over the hill is a good spot. I've ALWAYS seen deer here. Not only deer but, big, big, bucks." "There will be very thick evergreen trees for a while that we'll have to crawl through, slowly. When I part the trees, you will see a fence. Don't worry about the fence. There's lots of fences out in these parts. Have your guns ready. If the deer are in this area, we'll see them here. Remember, shoot the BIG bucks."

Joe parted the trees and there was a WHOLE HERD of deer out there. A 10 pointer, an 8 pointer, and smaller bucks and does. Joe said, "Don't miss." As they were "lining up" through the fence. The taller hunter said, "Hold it, Hold it!!!" "There's a sign posted here that says, GAME FARM, KEEP OUT!"

"What are you pulling here, Joe?" Joe said, "Its not a game farm, it's only got deer in there. You wanted a deer didn't you? There they are!!!"

One of these hunters came back, that night, to the bar and told us this story. We then asked, "Where is Joe Weasel now?" He answered, "I'm not sure. The last that I saw of him, my partner was chasing him through the woods somewhere near that "Polish Deer Blind."

Chapter 2

An Unforgettable Character ….. Penny

His real name was Joseph, although, I never heard
anyone call him anything but Penny. He came to Iron
Mountain as a child. At that time, he couldn't speak,
write, or read any English. Penny told me that he self-
educated himself to do all of those things in English.
There still was a little Italian accent to his speech,
though.

He was my Father-in Law's best friend. Both Italians
from Iron Mountain, they hunted at the Big Buck Camp,
approximately 60 miles north of the city, with six other
Italian partners.

His life was a real success story. A self-motivated
worker, with no particular skills other than a lot of
personal drive, he started in Iron Mountain as a worker in
a gas station. As soon as he could, he bought that gas
station, working many long and late hours himself rather
than having to pay out wages.

The mining trains ran through the city and near his
station. He said, "Hey, I knew they had to run on some
type of fuel, so I checked with them and asked how they
buy their fuel." "I figured that I could beat that price by
contracting semi-loads as they needed it. I sold it direct
from out of the semi to the trains. No storage tank cost."

He then bought four and five more gas stations, one at a time. Years later, he told me, with an emotional tear in his eye, "Only in America could someone arrive here with nothing and have the opportunity to become a millionaire." Italians are emotional people and Penny was no exception.

No one would ever think, though, that he had any more money that the average guy carrying a dinner pail. After all of those daily, long hours of work, you'd think he'd have slept on the weekends. No....., he was the first guy up at the camp plowing snow or the first guy out the door to go rabbit or deer hunting.

He and my Father-in-law were laughing it up at camp one day and telling the story about the time they were shooting woodcock alongside of a ridge. They were walking down a logging trail at the bottom of this ridge. There was a lowland swamp on one side of the trail and the ridge on the other. "It was unbelievable!" he said. "Towards sundown, the woodcock were flying out of that lowland swamp to the top of the ridge."

They were having a ball! The shooting time was running out (say it was at 4:30 PM) so Penny said, "Set your watch back 15 minutes." They both set those watches back about five or six times and kept shooting. Then, along came Coppo, the Game Warden. Coppo drove up and told them that they were shooting after the legal hour and now they were in trouble. "Penny replied, "No we're not. Check the time on our watches. Coppo did. He also checked his own and was a little confused. Two watches said O.K. but his didn't.

Before he could do much more thinking about it, Penny said, "Coppo, don't worry. Anyone can have a watch like yours that don't keep good time." "Come with us to camp and have some spaghetti and wine." Coppo quickly forgot about the watch problem and went to camp with the guys. He said, "Well, it does seem near supper time."

I saw Coppo in their camp many times. He'd always arrive at dark or suppertime. Someone would see his car pull in and say, "Here comes Coppo!" When he'd open the door and come in, everyone had a smile for him as if they were looking forward to seeing him. He always had darting eyes that danced around like he was looking for someone in a police lineup.

This camp had excellent cooks. If you liked pasta with a touch of garlic, garlic bread, and red wine, this was the place.

Everyone played cards after that big meal. Coppo would also play. I watched his eyes as he looked around. He looked like he wanted desperately to pinch someone. He looked very uneasy as he played. He probably though, he had a camp full of violators but couldn't find any reason to make a pinch.

Coppo probably knew most their tricks but couldn't prove a darn thing, and hey, why cut off such good meals? I later asked Penny, why they seemed to encourage him to keep coming to the camps? Penny said, "Hey Bob, its better to have him inside here where we know where he is." Then, when Coppo would leave the camp, Penny would watch him through the window and say, "Hey Boys, we're still one step ahead of Coppo."

For all of Penny's gained wealth, a stranger would never pick him out from anyone else at camp. He worked at the camp chores as hard as two people, never bragged himself better than anyone else, and I don't know of anyone that didn't like him. Even the local Priest would come to the camp just to eat, visit, and play cards (to eat was an understatement. These meals were feasts). Everyone there seemed genuinely pleased to have him as a guest and he seemed well relaxed and enjoyed their company.

Penny was as close to any "Godfather" figure that I ever saw. Other Italians went to him when they needed help with something. "Someone in City Hall was giving them trouble, or so they thought," Or, someone needed money desperately to pay a bill, etc. Penny helped them out. Most of it was communications. He listened and seemed to say the right things.

I felt privileged to have him call me his friend …………..

Chapter 3

The Screaming Eagle Deer Camp

"Look at that sign. CAMP SCREAMING EAGLE. Do you know those guys? Can we stop there? I'll bet they're veterans. Probably paratroopers if its called 'The Screaming Eagles.", "Can we visit them?" My partner, Vic, "a died in the wool" veteran, said on the way to our camp.

I said with a smile, "You think that they're veterans, hey? I'll take you over to visit there another time after it gets real light or real dark out. I never take a chance on them mistaking you for a deer or bear in the hazy light."

Their's is quite a camp. It has about 12 regular members and a few that tumbles in at any time. I was there early one season and saw most of them arrive. These are guys where their wives normally dominate them all year and they get this one, big, release "on their own" at deer season.

I was sitting with Red in front of the window, having a cool one, where we could watch down the road. Pretty soon, Gene's pickup came in, splashing through the puddles and stopped quickly, by the horizontal telephone pole laid there to keep the trucks, I think, from hitting the camp.

Gene jumped out of his truck all wide-eyed and a big smile. He has big eyes anyway. It seemed like he leads a "Clark Kent" life at home, (Yes dear, no dear, etc), but when he got to the camp, the chains were off and he thought he could be Superman.

The camp has a ½ barrel on tap set about 5 feet into the camp from the door and a pretty well stocked bar. This camp always has enough supplies to outlast a month-long blizzard.

A few hellos and Gene started drinking. He said, "Don't bother me, boys. I've waited all year for this." He was going at it like he had a mission. Like a camel forting up to go across a desert. We ignored him and greeted the other guys as they arrived. They looked at me, a little suspicious, but any friend of Red's was a friend of everybody.

The camp has six double bunks, a sofa, and a few good chairs you can sleep on. The early guys were claiming the best bunks and didn't want to sleep with "Snoring Tom." "Put him on the top bunk where all the good smells go," Russ said.

Their camp has many pictures of "Screaming Eagles" on almost every wall. Thus, it's named THE SCREAMING EAGLES. The guys all had to work the beer tap with Gene, who was starting to sound like he could "lick the world!" The beer was flowing as more hunters arrived. Moss, Curly, and Vern, came in a Ford Ranger, built for two. These guys are all huge. They were jiving Moss about his poor driving and he told them, he couldn't turn the steering wheel proper because their bellies were rubbing on it.

Red, who really owns the camp, said, "Let me tell you a story about those three guys from two years ago. That was the first year that Moss hunted with us." " The three of them were up here alone for a few days, the second week. They drove to Escanaba. Curly and Vern said they knew a good place to socialize so they stopped there and had a few. Then Curly and Vern told Moss to sit tight and wait for them as they were going to check on some girls.

Moss said that he waited for 3 hours for them. Finally, he decided to drive back to camp alone. He figured that those guys would find a ride somehow.

Moss told me that he was sound asleep back at camp when someone was tapping him on the shoulder to wake up. He turned around and here was a good-looking woman looking at him about a foot from his face. He thought, "Lordy, Lordy, did I go back to the wrong camp?" Then he could hear strange voices coming from the main room. He said, "Just stop and think how you'd of felt in this situation." Then Vern and Curly came in laughing. He said they brought two girls and two guys back with them. They treated them to their open bar for the ride back.

Moss said, "I thought that I was a tough guy, but I was so embarrassed that I put my head under the pillow and pretended to be sleeping."

This camp is so big that it has a special room with a long table and many chairs for card playing and eating (in that order). The worst snorer sleeps in there too, on a single bed. He didn't seem to mind so he must "rock the rafters" as Red put it.

Gene looked like he was "past full" and was now sitting down on a kitchen chair. His eyes looked a little different. They were really wide open and his mouth was open. He started to say, "me-me-me-me-me." Someone said, "He's starting with the me-me's again." It seemed like the only word he could say.

These guys really do get some big bucks. Red owns eight 40's and they have some very good deer blinds scattered around on them. They bait well and see a lot of deer.

I asked Red, "What do they call a good season?" He said, with a smile, "When no one shoots the camp or a hole in a car fender." Last year, Curly shot a hole in the back fender of a new Buick. It was parked over there, between those two evergreens and he said he saw that black fender and thought it was a bear." (I told Vic, thats why I go over there at full light or total darkness with good headlights.)

Gene started again, "me-me-me-me," so someone said, "He got like that from drinking…. Fight fire with fire. Give him another drink." Then he got louder and said, "ME-ME-ME-ME!!" They gave him another shot and he was quiet. Red said, "He gets like that every year." Jay stood in front of him staring intently, and said, "He sounds a little selfish with that, 'me-me-me-me', all the time."

Red then told them to "Put an army blanket around him and set him and the chair on the cold porch. The fresh air should be good for him." Gene started, "Help, Help,

Help, me-me-me-me." Vern figured that was doing the trick as he was talking more already.

I looked at him in that cold air and it looked like rigamortius was starting to set in. Red felt a little concerned to and told them to "Bring him in, boys. He can sleep sitting in a chair tonight, or else, he'll be hollering that he sees 'screaming eagles' again." Everyone seemed to be enjoying every minute of it.

The camp also has a good-looking female mannequin. Red said, "You can imagine the laughs we've had with that....taking pictures with it and some of the guys that fall off to sleep." I was thinking, in a camp like this, you'd be afraid to fall asleep.

When Vic and I got back home, he told my wife, "We're going to stop in on the 'Screaming Eagles' camp this deer season.' She said, "Humph! It seems like someone is always screaming over there." I smiled and thought....but I never seemed to hear any unpleasant screams. No, those "Screaming Eagles" aren't paratroopers. They are just a camp that is happy when they DON'T see "Screaming Eagles" after the lights are turned off.

Chapter 4

A Camp Full Of Game Wardens – Holy Wah!!

How would you like to open a camp door and find the camp all full of game wardens? John, a friend of mine, is a retired game warden. Of course, he is a hunter and fisherman like the rest of us. Anyone, who has spent that many years in the outdoors on that type of job, has to love it.

He is a member of a deer camp near Manistique, that by nature, happens to be all game wardens. John was telling me some stories of times that visitors happened to come there by accident and didn't know this was a game wardens' camp.

This one time, two young guys drove into their camp one night during hunting season. They knocked on the door, were asked to come in, and said they wanted directions to Camp Hi-ball. Before John could answer, they discovered from the clothes hanging around, that they were game wardens!

The first young guy shouted, "Holy Wah!! It's a camp full of game wardens!" and he backed up two steps. John said, "Its interesting to see the reaction of people when they discover that you're a warden, let alone a whole camp full. You can imagine what runs through someone's mind. It's like meeting a room full of income tax auditors and trying to carry on a conversation. Your thinking, I don't want to say anything to trigger a tax audit.

Coppo, the warden in the Ralph-Felch area (North of Iron Mountain) would frequently visit my father-in-law's deer camp and have a meal or play cards with the guys. But....you could sense the tense atmosphere and guarded stories then. When a camp hunter came in from hunting, someone would meet him at the door and in a low voice say, "Coppo's here." That would be passed to everyone as they came in.

I honestly never seen anyone of these camp members violate a game law. Yet, that was the uneasy feeling that they had with Coppo.

After he'd leave, someone would say, "That Coppo would pinch his own mother." I visited the warden's camp and noticed that like any camp, they had all ages of hunters there. One young warden looked in such good shape that I believe he could have outrun my dog.

They talked about all of the new equipment that they have: a night sight to see a person in total darkness, a hand-held device to find a violator hiding in the dark or a wounded deer after dark, listening devices to hear someone walking a 40 away.

I said, 'Its surprising anyone would violate if they knew what they were up against. One warden told me, "Its like going to the Casino. You think your going to win but it doesn't always happen. Sometimes, WE hit the Jackpot!"

They were talking over a lot of poor written game laws. It seems that these laws are written so that it is difficult to make an absolute arrest on someone. I was thinking, thank God for that! Its nice to know that the single hunter can still go to trial by your peers (jury) and explain your side of the story. Just maybe, you were innocent.

But, game wardens are human too. The ones that I personally know, are very nice people. They love the outdoors and the camp life. We have to appreciate their role of responsibility the same as a traffic cop, school principal, teacher, anyone else with the responsibility of authority. As long as they use reasonable common sense, the average sportsman can be happy to see them come down the trail.

Chapter 5

Camp Deer Run....
(Recently Re-named, CAMP ROAD KILL!!)

We should have known better. We had visited there before....The Camp Deer Run boys invited us over for venison steak on the 2nd day of deer season. They said they'd fry up three hindquarters.

We had good reason to be suspicious. One year, they invited us over to drink. After we got going, they said, "By the way, we need a little help cutting the wood pile up." Another time, it was "Would you mind making the cedar swamp drive and we'll post. We're allergic to cedar.'

John (from our camp), said, "If we go, guys, keep on your toes to tell them we have to go right back if they come up with a work detail. They never return the favor."

Their camp is different. Really different....Bill said, "The last time that I was there, the camp was so dirty that I think the mice slept outside."

Maybe we SHOULD have known better, but, we were curious why they were so generous with the deer steak on the second day of the season.

They were a dirty lot. Pete, who's nickname was Spot, (We figured because he always had dirt spots on his hands and face) said he'd volunteer to do the dishes because he needed to wash his hands anyway. I started to think quickly, what shots did I have this year? Flu? Lockjaw? Distemper?

They were all jiving Tom, another member of their camp, when we came in. They said Tom missed his wife so bad that he must be letting off a mating scent at his deer post. The does won't even stop to linger by his apple pile. They said he keeps reading those old camp Playboy magazines and pacing the floor. After this meal, they were going to send him home "for the cure."

We all sat down at their long table. I quickly asked for a paper plate, "To make dish washing easier." It didn't work....I got one of those semi-clean plates and a big smile for wanting to be so helpful.

There were mounds of food. It reminded me of pictures of the knights eating in King Arthur's Court. A bowl of fruit, a huge plate of homemade bread, beans and really large platters of venison and fried onions.

Everyone started eating and no one was saying too much. Steve, from our camp, leaned over to me and said, "Notice some of the meat is darker and seems to taste blood shot. Steve said, "Hey, how come you didn't cut off the blood shot meat before you cooked it?"

Spot was beaming. He said, "We're just sharing our good luck with you boys. Vern and Charley found two nice road-kill deer yesterday. Don't know how long they were dead but with onions and garlic, they don't taste bad."

"We didn't want to tell you where we got them ahead of time because some people might be more particular....eat up!"

Steve rolled his eyes and whispered, "Eat a lot of bread. There's no way they could have got THAT with their bumper." Pete said, "You boys are in for another treat. I made a homemade pie for this meal." We thanked them but said we were so full that we couldn't eat anymore."

On the way back to our camp we tried to guess what was in that pie. "Spot probably took some apples off of someone's bait pile."

John said, "You know, some nationalities eat dogs. I didn't see their old dog around when we were there." Bill smiled, "I don't think they'd cook it unless they killed it with their truck bumper." We all looked at each other and said, "WAH!!!" at the same time.

Their camp was renamed CAMP ROAD KILL after that by our crew and we vowed never to go there again at mealtime. The fried onions were good though............

Chapter 6

Sauna Troubles

Here's a story about my friend, Matti.

I stayed at the Brentwood Motor Inn at Marquette one weekend. The manager, Darrell, was a real friendly guy. We were exchanging fishing stories over his office counter and he said that he fishes almost every day.

After some good conversation, I settled down in a lawn chair overlooking parts of Lake Superior. I love Menominee but driving from a 90° temperature to a 55° temperature in Marquette made for nice sleeping.

I was just sitting on the second floor balcony by my room door when Matti (I'm not quite sure of the spelling of his last name but I think it was Kaukala) walked up and introduced himself. He said, "You're a writer, hey? Do you know what a sauna is? I can tell you a story about my cousin who came visiting last month. His name is Ralph Maki and he had his wife with him. I was a little suspicious of him when he introduced himself as Ralph. A Finlander named Ralph just don't sound right. I'd like to think that he is only part Finlander because he couldn't hold his beer good and he did odd things."

I got a chair out of the room for him and he started his story.

Let me tell you, he got me in trouble with my wife and the good ladies from the Women's Club. When it's my wife's turn to have them over, she normally asks me, "Matti, why don't you go somewheres else tonight." That's the one night she don't mind if I visit the boys down at Mili's bar.

What happened was, I invited him to go with me to Mili's when he spotted the sauna. He wanted to know how it worked, then he wanted to use it before we went to the bar.

I figured we could be on thin ice because the women would be sitting on chairs in the backyard near the sauna. I told my wife we'd use the sauna and leave quickly for downtown. She was nervous about that. Then she made me nervous. She said, "Matti, you smell like you could use that sauna but you do your business in there quickly and take that cousin of yours away from here. He looks like trouble to me."

That Ada, she can tell stuff like that ahead of time. She was making soup from home-canned Ludifisk and another lady was bringing over sandwiches left over from her daughter's wedding last week. I figured the ladies would only eat a little bit of that and try to fool each other by saying they are on diets.

Well, there they were. All bringing a chair and sitting in a big circle in the backyard and in sight of the sauna.

I told Ralph, we'd sneak a case of beer into the sauna to drink before they all got comfortably settled in. We did that and were feeling real good. Plenty of beer, a nice sauna, and Ada would never know.

Was I ever wrong. Remember I told you that cousin Ralph didn't look to plumb, kind of like a brick short of a load. After we did some honest drinking, he wanted to know the proper way to take a sauna. I was just satisfied being in there away from those women but I told him anyway.

I said, "We make a fire, pour water over the stones to make steam, take off our clothes, sit down, have a beer, switch yourself with those cedar twigs, pour more water for more steam, drink another beer, and when you feel done, run outside and roll in the grass to cool your body. Then go back in and drink the rest of the beer.

I was right. That Ralph, maybe from drinking in the heat or maybe because that's the way he is. He couldn't get the sequence down of how I just explained to take a sauna. The poor guy drank a beer, took off his clothes, drank another beer, and ran outside and rolled naked out on the lawn. He rolled right into the middle of that bunch of women.

The women tried to handle it calmly. One said, "Looks like he's taking that Viagra." Another, "Where do you get that Viagra?" Another, "I wish my Eino had that much energy. Look at him roll!"

All this time, Ralph, sensing he was "In the frying pan" closed his eyes and rolled back into the sauna. He said, "Matti, I need a beer after that." I congratulated him on rolling back in like he was supposed to do. Then we

27

heard, BANG, BANG, BANG, like someone was driving nails into the sauna.

Ralph looked through a crack and said, "Yeah, it's our wives. They are nailing the door shut." Ralph said, "You know those cedar twigs you slap yourself with, Matti? I think your wife wants to help you. She's sitting on a chair by the door with a BIG twig in her hand. In fact, it looks like a baseball bat.

That Ralph, we must have lost 10 pounds each by the time we got out of there the next day.

Chapter 7

Friends, And, A Women's Touch At Camp

I think that sometimes we take good friends for granted. There's nothing I enjoy more (well, there's ONE thing more) than a day with good friends.

Our camp has been blessed with good friends. You can rely on any one of them to do whatever is necessary without being told or wanting to take credit for it.

The first guy up there will fill up the wood boxes (Yeah, boxes, we burn a lot of wood), and does what else might need doing.

I can remember asking my Dad once how come he had so many good friends. He thought for a while and then said, "I guess if you're cheerful and helpful to others, it must become contagious."

This last deer season we had two friends from Wisconsin (one from Wausaukee and one from Marinette) come up to the camp just to be together. One, Carl, stayed for three days. He bought a non-resident license for this, although he owns some of the best hunting land in the Wausaukee area. The other, Dave, I had a feeling would have done the same thing but he just finished a triple bi-pass surgery a few months before and couldn't stand the gun recoil to this shoulder yet. Vic, another non-resident, has been with us now for three seasons.

What do guys do at camp other than, of course, hunting and things related to hunting? Well, we made an apple pie one night (we have no famous cooks in camp.) Everyone peeled and cut apples. One read the directions and it turned out perfect. The deer were shorted of some of the better apples at the bait pile because of this.

Then we made chili. This might sound like "peanuts" to you ladies, but to us we were stepping into a bold, new, frontier as far as we were concerned. We notice that chili was selling for $2.50 for a small bowl at the nearest pub. "We can make chili. Let's try." The same procedure....some cut up onions, lots of onions, and complained why someone else got the easy job of just stirring the pot. That didn't turn out bad either. I think the guys talked and bragged about that cooking as much as they did about deer hunting (and they are no slackers at the deer stories.)

Fr. Tim, my nephew, also a parish priest and hunter, living in Engadine was in camp for the second weekend of the season. We had a famous first. Fr. Tim gave a Mass in camp for the hunters. Talk about a camp with everything!

I saw Carl, from Wausaukee, later, in Fleet Farm in Green Bay. It's rare that we'd ever meet in Green Bay. The first thing he talked about was that apple pie that we made at camp and talked about coming back again next year.

I told him that he could buy a non-resident doe license for $30.00 rather than paying the $100.00 for the non-resident buck license. (He can only hunt for part of the first week as he goes to his own camp in Wisconsin beginning of our second week's season.) Carl said, "Oh no. I'll hunt for a buck. I just enjoy being up there. To watch the sun rise up over those evergreens and the hardwoods, having partridge walk around your blind, and, of course, watching for a big buck is an experience that's hard to beat." "We'll have to get that 'Big Swede' (Dave) to stay longer next year."

These are generous guys. One brought a case of good cheer, a bushel of good apples, a hundred pounds of shelled corn, and about 20 lbs. of meat. This was over and above what he insisted on paying for being there for 3 days.

A WOMAN'S TOUCH AT CAMP: I was up to camp alone one weekend when my brother-in-law, John, came visiting. He looked around and said, "Jeeze, you better hang up some stuff and straighten things up here. Do a little cleaning." I looked around and started to agree with him. Then, I thought, I guess what we really need is the gentle hand of a woman telling us, "Hang up that coat, make the bed, etc." Then I caught myself, "WHOA, WHOA!! This is one of the reasons that I enjoy coming up here. To relax, walk around in your shorts when the wood heater climbs to 80°, etc."

The camp….or, MAN'S LAST CAVE, we can still do what we want there and not feel inhibited. (When your wife doesn't come up, that is.)

I looked out the window and gazed fondly at the different wildlife moving around out there. Then, I thought of the very first weeks that my wife and I spent at camp together. We were just married. This was one of the first "Woman's Touch" at camp.

I believe it was a Thanksgiving week. She cooked a huge meal that included a big and beautiful pumpkin pie. We ate the meal and then got to the pie.....I'll tell you, people say that love is blind. You'll do anything to please a new wife when you're in love, but try like I did, I couldn't swallow any of that pie. It looked normal. There was some type of spice in it that tasted like a dentist's Novocain. LOTS of Novocain. (I, at this writing, asked her if she remembered that pie and what that overload of spice was it in. She said it was cloves, LOTS OF CLOVES.)

After a good share of diplomacy on my part, and a few tears on hers, I then put that whole pie outside on a stump for the wild animals. I figured they ate anything. After dark, we heard a lot of commotion out by that stump.

We got up and shined a light on it. There was a family of raccoon milling around it. The biggest one was grunting and squealing to the small ones. It then picked up the pie (tin and all) and dumped it upside down. It started to jump on the pie tin, at the same time talking to the young ones. I could just imagine what it was saying. "If you EVER run across something like this again in your life....." They all looked at it, backed away, and left.

In the morning, two squirrels ran to the pie. They actually started to EAT it. Then one bounced around like it had a seizure and got the diarrhea. The other took heed and stopped eating. The sickest looking one ran for a tree and climbed up. Now if you ever watch a normal squirrel climb a tree, they leap at it and automatically, run up its side like we walk on the ground. Not this time. That poor squirrel leaped at the tree, went up about 8 feet, burped, and slid back down those eight feet to the ground. He left scratches on the way down like a kid dragging his fingernails on a chalkboard. There appeared to look like an "oil slick" on the tree trunk where he slid down. Probably diarrhea.

I looked out, very serious, at those poor animals and thought….WAH! That could have been me! Those squirrels gave up trying to climb a tree for safety and slowly, ever so slowly, went into the woodpile to spend the day. I could have sworn that I heard one say, HOLY WAH! from under that woodpile.

My wife and I get along exceptionally well, but I shiver anytime I see her attempt another pumpkin pie. She laughs about it now and says, "oh, loosen up. I know how to make it the right way now." I look at her curiously and wonder what she means by the "right way now." I didn't see a raccoon around the camp for two years after that pie ordeal.

Now when Thanksgiving comes around and the kids come home for that "Wonderful, home-cooked meal" she'll say, "I'm going to make a couple of homemade pumpkin pies" to me. Feeling it's my duty to protect, at least, the kids, I'll say, "No, no, make apple pies. The pilgrims had apple pies." We really love your apple pies." She'll look at me out of the corner of her eye then. She knows…..I can tell…………..She knows….Wah! I still shiver when I walk past someone in a restaurant and they're eating a piece of pumpkin pie.

My kids laugh about it. I told them this story some time ago. Randy, my oldest son, will come home and say, "Tell my son the pumpkin pie story, Dad." No way! I know better. I only tell that story now when it's a "men's day only" at camp and we're all telling camp experiences.

Besides, it's more believable up there where you can see the stump, the trees, and imagine those animals. The kids now laugh about it until they get tears in their eyes. Then I look out the window and still think of those poor animals. Yeah, it could have been ME.................!

Chapter 8

The Great Turkey Chase

I was riding down the Menominee River road, Monday, and saw something interesting. There were 3 tom turkeys chasing a single hen turkey. They looked like two younger toms and the third tom looked like a 30 pounder. He had a beard that was about a foot long.

He would run full speed to catch that hen, would trip on that long beard, fall down, roll on his side, and get up quickly to try and win the chase. All three toms would periodically run sideways to pick at the competitor who was "closing the gap" on the hen.

They'd each seem to change places for the lead when this would happen. The hen looked like she knew her stuff. She'd run, but just fast enough to stay about 5 feet ahead of her romantic pursuers.

A tom would catch up and immediately make a beautiful fan with his tail and strut his wings. The other toms would then run right past him to try to be number one. The foolish "struter" then would drop his feathers back to normal and run like heck to get back into the race.

The toms were their own worst enemy. They'd pick at each other to slow up the advance of each other. The hen seemed to be enjoying all of this. She'd look behind once in a while to check how close they were, and speed up or slow down when she had to,...........just enough.

That old tom with the long beard would run, trip on his beard, fall, roll over, get up quickly, and continue the chase. This all took place after the four turkeys walked timidly across the road in front of my car.

They went across the yard of an elderly couple. The hen kept looking at the picture window in the house as she slowly and coyly ran. Then I saw this older lady in the window smiling and cheering the hen on.

The two young toms closed in but instead of satisfying her, they chose to pick at each other (probably still trying to be number one.)

After watching them for an impatient, long time, she made a half circle toward "long beard." He caught her eye and stumbled, stepped on his beard, fell, rolled over, got up, but ran toward her like his life depended upon it.

Finally he caught up. It looked like she also slowed to a walk. He put his back to me and spread all of his feathers (it looked like an old Indian war bonnet), and you couldn't see either one because of the huge mass of feathers. No one was running away.

I had my young neighbor with me. His mother asked him if he seen anything exciting on the trip. He said, "Sure, four turkeys chasing each other." I smiled.....Yeah, just wait until he gets older.

Chapter 9

Deer Camp – We're Ready!!

Last weekend I was hitching up a log splitter that I borrowed from a friend of mine in Menominee, "Baker Don." He wasn't home and the safety bolt to secure the trailer hitch (after you clamp it down) was missing.

I noticed his neighbor roto-tilling his garden so I went over and asked to borrow a piece of wire (old yooper trick) to secure the hitch. He said, "Sure, come on into my garage." After he gave me the wire, we introduced ourselves and he said, 'Aren't you the U.P. Rabbit?" I told him, "Yes." He was Jerry Swanson and he smiled and told me he reads my article each month in the "Porky." He said, "Hey, you missed writing one a few months ago." I honestly told him that it was Mike's fault (our faithful publisher/editor), as he switched over a different place or type of printing and they left out a few articles. (I write a monthly article in a U.P. magazine under the pen name, U.P. Rabbit.)

I asked Jerry if he read my book, 'Humorous Stories from the U.P. Hunting Camps." He never heard of it so he asked where he could get a copy. I told him, "Right in my truck.' So now Jerry's got an autographed copy. I've got room in my Ford Ranger for me, my wife, and a pile of books. Hope you enjoyed it, Jerry.

My brother-in-law and his boys came down from Kingsford to help split 3 full cords of oak that I had piled and waiting for them.

I got to the camp (in Lake Township) about 10:00 AM. They had a fire going in camp and cut about another ½ cord of wood to finish what was left before my saw burned out last weekend. We started up the splitter at 10:00 AM and finished the pile at 12:45. Finished means that they also wheeled it into the woodshed, stacked it and piled two rows across the camp's 20 foot long porch.

These guys are younger and never stopped working. I limped away from that splitter with a very sore back. My back felt like a double-jointed Rapala fish plug. I seemed to move two ways when I walked.

We went into the camp for dinner and I was afraid to sit down. I had to cook and wasn't sure I would be able to stand up again. One good thing, I can cook and those guys can eat. Two pounds of spaghetti (our Italian background) red sauce, a pound of hamburger thrown in for "body", two loaves of garlic bread, red wine and a homemade apple pie.

After all that work, we settled down at the table. These boys were hungry. All I could hear was the slurping of sucking up that spaghetti and see a fine spray of red sauce as we finished those two pounds of spaghetti. No one talked while they ate. They worked hard and ate fast. One guy looked up sheepishly, and he looked like someone shot him. He had a lot of that red sauce on the front of his shirt. I wondered what else they did fast? (And I had the reputation of being called the Rabbit?....)

We all pushed back our chairs and went into the front room to "sit on something softer." After about a half-hour of bragging about which one of us was going to shoot a big buck, John said, "What else do you want us to do while we're here?" I said, "How about cutting up that pile of cedar slabs to use for starter wood?" He said, "Let's go, boys." Everyone tackled that like they were just starting to work.

I was grateful to lean over and hold the bundles down on the sawhorse as they cut them with the chain saw. Well, SOMEONE had to hold it. In about a ½ hour, it was cut and stacked in the woodshed. I looked around and thought, "Thank God for making good relatives."

Good naturally, I told them that I'd shoot their deer for them for all the help. They smiled. Holy Wah! Those guys are half sportsman and half timber wolf. Their fast in the woods and don't miss any deer sign as they go.

I took them for a walk to my deer blind (in our neck of the woods, it's considered a high privilege for someone to show you their deer post and explain its finer points.) Mine is located on a high ridge overlooking the edge of a cedar swamp, a stand of young popples, small and large evergreen trees, and some old pine stumps. I always felt that it would be a good spot to place a Gatling gun in case I was overrun by a big herd of bucks on opening day.

The boys pointed out two new tree scrapes made by bucks since last weekend. Steve showed me one stand of small willows that were "buck scrapped" and explained that it was done by a large buck. Probably a 6 or 8 pointer or larger because of the way it scrapped so many bushes together.

I figured that he was getting to be somewhat of a B.S.'er like his Dad or just maybe he knew what he was talking about. After all, he ate all of that spaghetti and my sauce and he was still standing up. He must know his stuff and I had pictures in my mind of that big buck coming past me on opening day. Ya, I believe him.

I got a new box of those Winchester Silvertip 30/30 shells and now I should be all set. I like those Silvertips because they don't flatten out on the ends if you have them in the gun's magazine a few times, and besides, they're kind of pretty.

Well, we finished the last, big chore with that wood splitting before deer season. It's a lot of work but there's no better warmth than heat from wood when you come in from sitting out in the cold.

Good luck on the hunt.

POST-SEASON NOTE: We all filled up with bucks. Two 8 – pointers, 3 spike-horns, and a fork-horn.

Chapter 10

Bill Rides His Buck
Or
The Buck "Didn't" Stop Here!!

It was the first day of the new deer season. The REAL rifle season in Michigan's U.P....November 15th....The date that most hunters remember better than their wife's birthday.

It was still dark in the camp. I heard Bill get up with his flashlight and turn on the light to start breakfast. Pretty soon, Vic got up to join him. I clenched my teeth together...Neither one of them could cook worth a hoot, but they both seemed happier than two coons in a corncrib.

These guys could burn bacon and eggs to a metal skillet like it was a part of a plan. When they'd scrap off a section of eggs and bacon stuck to that pan, I'd get flashbacks from those cooks that we had in the army.

Many of them signed up in the army as heavy equipment operators as promised by some recruiting sergeant. They seemed to actually detest having their hands clean to cook. These guys wanted to be operating a huge bulldozer or some such machine. Not serving up food that they had no interest in cooking to a lot of complaining soldiers.

Being that no one else in the camp wanted that job, anyway, the rest of us were smart enough to smile and eat a lot of bread with it.

The outside rays of light were just breaking through the dark sky. No one wanted to leave the camp too soon. Everyone, for one reason or another, were rubbing their bellies and hoping they could have a "movement" at camp, before they put on all of those clothes and had no facility out in the woods.

Contrary to what the national sports magazines say about the rugged sportsmen, those around our camp still like the luxury of a toilet even when he's in the woods. This job over, everyone quickly dressed and started to their posts before "shooting light" came up.

Dave and I were walking together. He leaned over and whispered, "Don't be too hard on the cooks. Like the army, they're making fighting men out of us. One meal like that and you want to go out and kill something." I looked back at Dave. He looked like he had fire in his eyes.

We all reached our posts with a little darkness to spare. We put out some fresh corn by our bait piles, quietly rearranged the cover within arms reach of the blind, put the gun up to our shoulders, and sighted at a tree in the distance. We want to be sure that with all the layers of clothes that we had on still allowed us, at least, that much freedom of movement.

Then we check our watches, for no apparent reason, and were as quiet and watchful as we could. My blind is a 40 and one half away from the nearest hunter from our group. Bill and Tim's blinds are on a high, hardwood ridge and within sight of each other. Personally, I don't like to hunt that close together for safety reasons. They both, however, each have excellent posts. They always see a lot of does each and normally two to three bucks on a good season.

Those hardwoods are big timber, scattered with huge broken treetops, periodically covering the ground. There is a mixture of beechnut trees on this ridge and of course, a lot of dead, downed wood. The deer and turkey seem to love those beechnuts as good as fresh corn.

This is a very long and high ridge. It probably extends for one half mile with its one end tapering off into a big cedar swamp.

Bill was in his blind and Tim quietly watching out of his own. Tim had put out a new deer lure. He placed it about 10 feet in front of his blind. He said it was called, "Wild Passion." Vic also decided to hunt the ridge for the first day so he made a "quick blind" near the cedar swamp. (On making a "quick blind", you gather whatever natural treetops are around you, form them up around a tree that you lean against and you have a "quick blind." It at least breaks your solid body form from whatever wildlife passes by.)

There were many things that happened on that ridge that day. Tim told this story later. About 9:00 AM, he thought he could hear Bill walking up to Tim's blind from his backside. He said that the dead maple leaves are about 8 inches thick up there, so it's easy to hear someone walking. He did think that it was odd for Bill to come walking over to his post at such prime hunting time.

The heavy steps kept coming to his blind and Tim was thinking, "I wish he didn't make that much noise so he didn't scare the deer." After all, the deer could move through those leaves like a silent wind. Most of the time you had to actually have to see them rather than hear them.

Tim excitedly told everyone in camp, "I waited till it seemed like Bill was only 20 feet behind my blind. Then I stood up and looked around the back to see why he was coming over at this prime shooting time."

"When I poked my head around the corner, I couldn't believe it! There stood a 14 point buck not 20 feet away! I swear that it had 14 points as it was so close, I counted them!" My gun was well out of reach as I thought it had to be Bill coming.

"The buck and I saw each other at the same time. He had to be attracted to that new buck lure that I put out. That would explain why he was making so much noise walking in the leaves and why he came up so close."

The buck immediately turned and ran in the direction of Bill's blind. Bill said that it was making so much noise running in those leaves that he easily heard it coming…. He said, "It came crashing through broken treetops like they weren't even there. It could have awakened a hunter from a sound sleep."

He saw all of its many tines reflecting from the sun on to its huge set of antlers. It was running "full out' to try and disappear into a bushy, wild hay marsh in front of Bill's blind.

Now, Bill swung into action! He knew that he had to react fast! To react slowly meant a sure case of "Buck Fever" for Bill and maybe not even get a chance at this monstrous buck. He said that he shot his .300 Savage, lever action, rapid fire. He took the best aim that he could as it ran through those hardwoods. He shot five times, then his gun was empty. Bill looked at the ground and there were three empty shells and two full ones. He said, "Those two must have been duds but I was shooting as fast as I could work that lever."

The buck COLLAPSED and fell still. Tim said that when that fast shooting started, he dived to the floor of his blind and stayed there until he was sure Bill's gun was empty. Bill walked over to the deer and saw it lying there dead –still! He was beside himself! A 14 pointer and on the first day! He allowed himself a little time to shake and settle down.

Then he set his gun against the tree, took off his coat, pulled out his knife, walked over about 6 feet to the buck, and straddled it. He planned to field dress it himself. Well, he took a hold of the deer's front leg to turn it over and low and behold, that deer wasn't dead! Not by a long shot!

It jumped up and Bill grabbed a hold of the horns. The deer took off running back toward the big cedar swamp with Bill hanging onto its horns and half-riding and half-flying out in space behind it. He said that he thought it would fall down again and die. He wasn't about to give up that huge trophy easily.

Tim said, "They ran past my blind and it sounded like Bill was saying, 'Holy Mary, Mother of God....'" Then one of Bill's big swamper boots came off and was rolling down the ridge. "It sounded like he was really religious or else getting real desperate." The buck then headed downhill toward the swamp and right past Vic's blind.

Vic saw them coming and shouted, "Jump Off!" "Jump off, so I can get a shot at it. Bill said later, "I wasn't going to let go and let someone else shoot my buck. Remember, I thought it was well hit and should be dropping dead any second." Seeing Vic, seemed to give the deer its second wind. It put on a burst of speed and was going hell-bent for the swamp.

It took nerve to hang onto those horns, but we figured anyone who cooked like he did, have a lot of nerve. The swamp looked like a solid mass of woods with no trail where that deer was headed. It leaped into the swamp ducking under a cedar tree that was uprooted. Poor Bill hit that horizontal cedar tree about belly high. It looked like he had his arms over the top of the tree and his feet were dangling below.

The deer disappeared into the swamp, never to be seen again. Later, we all agreed that it must have been "horn shot." That would explain knocking it out and its coming back to full life again with no blood trail.

Bill walked back up onto the hardwood ridge limping slightly from losing a boot and minor bruises from hitting the cedar swamp. He looked a little stunned, had an unusual smile, and said, "No one will ever believe that I was riding a deer today." Vic excitedly said, "If you would have got off of the fool thing when you went by me, I could have shot it."

Bill looked at him like he still wasn't quite sure that he really did ride that deer. Everyone teased Bill then back at camp. "All Bill needs to get his buck is a rock to knock it out, his knife to clean it, and ....let's chip in and buy him a saddle for next year's hunt."

Bill, by now, had his second wind and thought he'd come out of this somewhat of a hero. He said, "I tried to steer it closer to the camp so you guys wouldn't have to drag it so far...."

Another time, I was looking for a wounded spike horn buck that we shot during a heavy rain. There was, of course, no snow and any blood trail was immediately washed away. It was a real downpour. I walked higher on the ridge looking and Randy walked about ¾ of the way up. He jumped the deer as it was lying down.

The deer jumped up and ran past me so close that it pushed me back a few inches, similar to going past someone else down a crowded Casino bus isle. It was like a miracle that we found it again in that pouring rain and "Brought home the deer."

Hunting with Bill was no place for the meek or reluctant. You never knew what he'd do next. He still takes a lot of jiving from this experience, like, "Bill, your supposed to shoot them before you clean them."

Chapter 11

Two-Hunters In A One-Person Deer Blind

Jay, Son-in-law of Bill, wanted to go Black Powder hunting this particular Saturday in the worst way. His wife told him, "No, that's out of the question. My parents are coming over to visit for the day. You've got to get to know my Dad better anyway."

Now, Jay was thinking. There's more than one way to skin a cat. He said, "I planned on asking him to go hunting with me too. I've got that nice deer blind so he should be warm and comfortable. Besides, think how nice that will be. My Father-in-law and I,....alone....in a deer blind, visiting and enjoying each other's company, all day."

His wife thought that over and couldn't find any problems with it. Jay was still stuck with his Father-in-law so it didn't sound like he was getting away with anything. She said, "Well, if he really wants to go with you, I guess it would be O.K."

Jay smiled. It sounded like everyone would be happy and he would be hunting. No sitting in the front room watching TV and talking over football that he didn't like anyway. Bill was agreeable to go. He wasn't looking forward to those front room, "watch whatever you want to, Dear...." shows either.

Saturday came and Bill and his Son-in-law, Jay, were both happy and agreeable. They were riding up north to Jay's land. He previously put out deer corn (bait) in preparation for this hunt. Chances of getting at least one good shot looked very, very, good.

On arrival, they put out some more fresh, shelled corn and noticed deer tracks all over the place. Again, conditions looked VERY good. Now, you should know, Jay built that plywood blind to fit one person....himself. There was normally room in there for him and a pail of apples or corn and little else. It was, by anyone's standards "just right" for one person.

These guys arrived at high noon and were expecting the good shooting to start at dusk. "I had to sit on a pail turned upside down," Bill explained to me, "And, of course, Jay had the best seat. He also had the only gun."

After an hour of sitting and "moving around just a little" the blind started tipping heavily to one side. Jay said that he had pieces of 2x4 boards standing on edge under the blind to keep it from rotting on he ground. They weren't nailed to anything.

"Go easy when you move, Bill, or you might tip us over....Jeeze!" Bill said, "Move over a little will you?" Jay just looked at him. "I think that I'll take off my coat," Bill told him. Jay said, "Where did you plan on putting it?" Bill thought about that and said, 'I think I'll leave it on." "Did you bring anything to eat, Jay?" Jay sounded a bit disgusted and said, "We didn't come here to eat, we came to shoot a deer and....with my nice, new, Black Powder gun." Jay had never shot it yet.

After about two hours of sitting on that pail turned upside down, Bill said, "I have to make a nature call." I asked Jay to open the door and let me out. God, my back was killing me from being hunched up in there like that.

Jay said, "You can't go outside now to do that. See….there's a flock of turkey walking into the corn pile right now. If you go out, you'll scare them away and probably they will scare away any deer that's nearby watching them."

Bill was now beside himself. He saw the turkeys out of the window but he really had to go….bad! Jay, trying to be helpful, said, "There's a coffee can in here somewhere for that purpose. Feel around for it. Use that and don't even THINK of going outside. Jay was a very serious hunter.

Bill, feeling the pain, said, "That blind was really small. You couldn't see the floor between them." He felt around frantically! Finally, he found it. He stood half way up (the blind had a very low ceiling) and that small building started to tip again….backwards!

He tried to figure out how he was going to do this. He couldn't even SEE the can, only that he knew he had it in his hand. Jay, getting nervous, said, "Sounds like your missing the can." Bill, "You got that right." "Whatever you do," said Jay, "don't go on me."

Bill, in an abnormal position, one foot against the front wall to prevent the blind from tipping, said, "Now I know how a dog must feel by a fire hydrant." Jay looked at him kind of annoyed but thankful that he was still dry.

Bill then sat down and said, "Move over a little." Jay moved his shoulders back and forth thinking "where"? What started out as a "bonding" between a Son-in-law and Father-in-law was now starting to get a little testy.

Bill said, "How about ME sitting on that nice seat for a while. I can feel a perfect ring cut into my bottom from this pail." Jay told him, "I'm the only one that can shoot this thing accurately." He smiled, then said, "I'm also trying something new with this gun to reach those bucks that won't come out of the swamp. It will be a surprise for you."

At this point, Bill told me that he didn't need anymore surprises. "Picture yourself needing at least three feet of space and having only a foot and one half to sit in. I was sitting on that pail, my bottom now numb, my arms around Jay's waist to balance myself and the blind, and my head resting over his shoulder." Jay glanced at me a few times. It was a good thing that we understood each other and the situation.

Just as we were getting numb all over, a few deer started to slowly come into the bait area. They were easy to see against the white snow. Bill thought, "Thank God! Shoot one Jay so we can go outside and straighten up."

Jay, very patiently, took his binoculars that he had hanging from a nail and looked over the prospects. He said, "there's a 6 pointer coming in and a bigger buck hanging back farther!" Bill, wanting to get out of there and straighten up, said, "SHOOT! SHOOT!"

Jay, looking over the deer, said, "No, the 6 pointer only has 3 points on one side and a single spike on the other.

We'll wait for the bigger one." Bill thought, damn, Jay went to Canada and shot a trophy Whitetail and now he thinks he's got to only shoot trophies. Bill again, said, "Shoot the first one!" Jay, "No, let them go and let them grow." (The new slogan of the U.P. sportsmen who want more trophy deer.) The first buck walked slowly away.

The bigger one, as they normally do, didn't step into the "clear shot zone." Bill said, "Let them go and let them grow....now you don't have any meat to show." Jay smiled, "Now, I'll show you my surprise. I put a triple charge of Black Powder down this barrel. This gun will reach out."

Bill in a panic, said, "No! No! Don't shoot that thing! It could explode!!!" Jay again smiling, knowing that Bill gets excited quickly, said, "Don't worry. Look how thick the metal is on this gun barrel. We should be able to put in all the powder we want. Besides, its all got to come out of the end of the barrel. Look at the killing power we'll have." Jay carefully slid the barrel out of the window and was squinting down the sights.

Bill said again, "Don't shoot that thing! I'm trapped back in here like a rat!" Jay pulled the trigger. A lot of things then, happened! "BALOOOM!!" and then, "PA-WANG!!!" Jay's eyes bugged out like golf balls. The shot somehow hit and bounced off the large propane tank to the side of the deer. The recoil of all that extra Black Powder ejected Jay, HARD!....through the back, plywood wall of the blind and out into the snow. The deer, of course, ran away.

The blind, for some reason, filled up with solid, black, smoke from all of that ignited Black Powder. Jay, with his eyebrows now burned off and his hunting cap smoking, shook his head to clear it. He said, "Are you in there, Bill?" Bill came out, appearing dazed, his face and clothes were all black from the gun powder. Only the whites of his eyes were the right color.

He said, "I can't hear a damn thing but there sure is more room in there now." On the way home, Jay, probably feeling a little sheepish, said, "This bonding between us is really nice. We'll have to go again.' "Next time, we can both go for a nice, long, ride on my snowmobile." Bill thought, "I wonder what he's got in mind? See if he can beat out a train at a junction?"

Bill, who is a barber, said, "I'm suppose to RELAX on my weekends. My nerves are so tight now that I'll probably cut someone shaving them on Monday." "What are you laughing about Jay?" Jay said, "I'm just thinking how lucky I am to have an electric razor."

Chapter 12

The Critters Living in Dad's First Camp

He had a total of three different hunting camps in his hunting career. Each one was an improvement over the previous one.

The first camp, in Menominee County, was bought out of an estate. It was closed up for possibly 5-8 years before he took ownership. It had a confusing "paper trail" to find the right relatives living in Arizona and convincing them to sell it. They inherited it and didn't seem interested in even selling it.

I guess he was so intent in owning it and the excellent hunting land (80 acres) that it was built on, that he wrote more letters than probably the people before him that tried to buy it.

With patience and perseverance, he succeeded in buying it. I don't think the relatives in Arizona had ever seen it. It was a log cabin. Upright logs with chinking between MOST of the logs. (A lot of the chinking had fallen out.) The floor was sagging in the middle. Another major repair job. The trim boards were mostly rotten and needed replacement.

There was a lot of steady repair work needed to bring it back to a comfortable use status. It never had any insulation but it had one huge, wood heater. In the fall and winter, that heater ate wood like that one hungry relative that everyone seems to have.

Friends of Dad's would stop in on the weekends. Some helped a little and some were just curious. One said, "You sure are lucky to have something different like this to do (repair the old camp) on weekends." My brother looked at me and said, "Ya, lucky us."

These weekend friends also were noticing the excellent deer hunting land that came with this camp. I'm sure Dad had read Mark Twain's *Tom Sawyer* and the story about painting the fence. Remember? Tom would say, "It sure is fun painting this fence," and his friends wanted to get in on it so they also painted the fence.

It wasn't long and he had an electrician friend, a carpenter, and two off-duty city firemen that were helping to recondition the old camp.

Now, buildings may be closed up and not used for a while by humans but that doesn't mean that they have no inhabitants. This camp had three animal holes dug under it on three different sides. He'd fill them in with stones and sand and the next week, they were dug open again. Dad then set a trap by each hole with a long wire staked away from the building.

The first weekend back, one of the holes was dug out wider and the trap chain was pulled under the camp. That hole was dug out big enough to hide a timber wolf. Dad wasn't taking any chances. He loaded up his single shot 12 gauge. Holding this in one hand with the hammer back and the trap chain in the other, he slowly tried to pull the chain and the trap out. There was a lot of resistance and ALL AT ONCE, a huge, and I mean HUGE, badger exploded out of that hole! Its teeth were lashing out and its huge, sharp claws were aimed at Dad. The badger leaped off of the ground at him and Dad pulled the trigger. Fortunately for him, he hit the badger dead center. For a few seconds there, it was him or the badger.

That was the first and only badger that I have ever seen in my lifetime in the Michigan woods.

Any wild animal can be vicious when it's cornered and this one was no exception. That took care of one hole under the camp. The next weekend, we slowly looked around the corner of the camp and there sat a good-sized skunk in a trap. It was sitting there as peaceful as if it was out sunning itself. Now how do you take a skunk out of a trap without getting yourself and the surrounding area all stunk up? Dad thought for a minute and then whispered, "If I can stand it up straight so it can't lift its hind end up, I don't believe it can spray."

I backed up and couldn't believe that he was going to try that. With a long pole, he slowly lifted the trap and the skunk's front end up into the air. Its hind feet were still on the ground. He then walked up closer, took a hold of the trap chain so he could keep the skunk's front end up off of the ground. As unbelievable as this is going to sound, this actually happened and is a true story.

He then untied the far end of the trap's chain and literally, WALKED OUT THE CAMP ROAD with that skunk walking about a foot alongside of him. The skunk's paw was still in the trap and at a distance, it looked like (similar) a small child walking and holding onto his hand!

That skunk's hind feet were touching the ground and evidently, it was impossible for it to spray being in that position. I know this may be hard to believe, but it's true. They walked together then, down the gravel road in front of the camp road, downhill about an acre, and then Dad tied the trap chain up onto a tree limb so the skunk had to stay in that same position.

He then came back to camp and got his .22 rifle. He went back and solved that skunk's problem. I don't think that there was any smell sprayed at THAT time. Later, like another weekend he went and retrieved his trap.

We then filled THAT hole with stones and dirt. The other trap never caught anything. We then sealed up that hole. Whatever used that hole may have watched the action with the skunk and thought, it too, would give up without a fight and clear out.

The one bedroom wall (the outside wall were logs, wood pieces to provide a straight inner wall, and a one inch thick layer of some type of 4' x 8' wall board, painted), had a large colony of bees in it one fall. You couldn't see them but somehow they got between the wall layers from the outside. They were about "head high" when you lied down on the first bunk. And, also, only about a foot away from your head. We'd hit the wall with our hand periodically to "rev them up." They'd buzz so loud that you'd swear they were going to explode through the wall.

That was my poor brother's bunk. I'd smile and knock on his wall, just to keep him alert. He'd wake up with his eyes wide open!

There were very few mice ever in this camp. Dad went after them with a passion. He always felt that they attracted snakes and he had no love for either one. He set mice traps, put out D-Con, mice "poison corn" bars, etc.. He have them a choice of whatever he could find on the market.

In the winter, (this idea actually works very well...and will catch as many mice as you have around.) He'd take a 5-gallon pail and place it on the enclosed porch. He'd spread a newspaper firmly across the top of the pail and tie it around the rim at the top of the pail with a length of string. Then he'd take a razor blade and cut 4 cuts from the center of the paper to almost near the rim of the pail (similar to cutting four pieces of pie). The very center cuts would be cut free, so, if a mouse ran across the top, the paper could bend in and the mouse would fall into the pail.

Now, to attract the mice, he hung a piece of cheese on a string extending down from the porch roof above, with the cheese over the pail's center but about 6 inches higher than the paper. You also had to place about 4 pieces of wood 1 – 2" wide, from the floor to leaning against the pail's rim. This gave the mice a natural "road" to scamper up the wood, reach the top of the pail, run across the paper after the cheese, and end up in the pail.

It's a foolproof mousetrap that never needs resetting to catch the second, third, or how many.

The plastic pail walls are straight, slick, and high enough that they don't escape.

The "biggest critter" that surprised Dad in that camp happened on a weekend when he was there alone. He said that it was a wonderful fall day, so he left the front door and the screen door open. The mosquito season was over so this made a convenience for him to go in and out.

He said that he went into the camp, this one particular time, and he could sense something BIG, that he felt come in and was standing behind him. He had the stove lid open and was just putting in a piece of wood....

He turned around, slowly. Not knowing what it might be behind him....he had no weapon handy. When he looked, there stood a full-grown doe deer about 2 feet behind him. It came, noiselessly, through the open door.

Now he sweated out what to do next. He didn't want to frighten it and have it jump through a window. He slowly walked 6 feet to the kitchen cabinet and got some cookies. He gave it a cookie. It ate it just like a pet, he said. Then he held out another cookie and walked it back out the front door.

Dad later reasoned that someone probably befriended this deer at another camp or house. He never did see it again which adds a little more mystery to "THE CRITTERS LIVING BY THE CAMP."

Chapter 13

A Desperate Diner in Deer Season

I was invited to deer hunt with a very good friend of mind in his Northern Wisconsin camp last year....WAY north! We drove for 3 ½ hours to reach the camp. Carl had a very large and comfortable camp. As we pulled into the yard, I also noticed that he had a huge woodpile all cut and neatly stacked. This then was going to truly be a relaxing hunting trip.

We arrived three days before the opening day. Like Carl said, "It will give you time to adjust to the camp and scout your deer post." The four of us, Carl, Dave, Geno and I were all recently retired. We were looking forward to this time spent together as well as the hunting.

After settling our gear in the camp, Carl said, "Let's drive into a small town up here that I know. If you forgot to buy anything, you'll still get a chance now, before you need it." I remembered that I needed flashlight batteries so, it sounded like a good plan.

This small, northern town was crowded with deer hunters. Their bright orange clothes and very noticeable deer-skinning knives hanging from their belts set them apart from anyone else. They all seemed to be walking proudly, like they felt as though they were someone special. What the hey, ...WE WERE SOMEONE

SPECIAL! Guys on their own, for one or two weeks. Cooking and providing for themselves. This probably was the only time these men made their own beds and cooked their own meals. Most had a feeling of accomplishment but still were happy it was only for two weeks. You can eat most anything for two weeks and still survive.

We visited a neighboring camp on the way back from "town." This camp just finished washing their socks and underwear. They said that they never did this at home and were pleased of their results. Strange what "two week hunters" feel are unique experiences.

Back at camp, Carl showed everyone the "tricks" to lighting the gas lights. We then sat down and discussed who would be our best cook. Each one of us was a fair cook, so we decided that we'd all share that job.

"Guys," Carl said. "Tonight I'm going to take you to a tavern that's different from any that you ever went to back home. This place is REALLY different. You can decide for yourself if you want to eat in there. Remember it's always a learning experience to see something that you haven't seen before."

Knowing Carl, I figured this place HAD to be really something different. Remember we were a long ways north of our regular standards and things we took for granted. This remote and sandy country was a far distance from our homes and what we were used to.

We all loaded into Dave's van and with Carl's directions, drove from one back road to another. He told us that the tavern was about 15 miles from the camp. Every place

61

up there was a far distance apart. It seemed like Dave enjoyed hitting all of the potholes in the roads as we bounced up and down. Carl, half apologizing, said, "They don't have much gravel on these roads up here." Geno, looking out of his side window, said, "Yeah, and what there was, I think the partridge must have ate it all up."

We finally arrive at the tavern. It looked like most buildings up north, off the "Prosperity Path." The front of it had a faded out sign that said, "TAVERN AND EATS." Short and to the point. The parking lot was gravel with some pretty good-sized rocks sticking through. You had to drive in there slowly as there naturally were also some good-sized potholes.

A few "good ole boy's" pickup trucks were parked there. One was missing a tailgate, another a smashed-in grill with one headlight missing. Carl walked past it and said, "That's what they call getting your deer the hard way."

There were some rental cabins in the back and off to one side. From the grass grown up around them, it appeared like they were only used during the deer season. A few had cars parked between them.

We were all anxious to go inside. If Carl wanted us to come here, it had to be something really different. The door was hard to open. It looked like the building shifted over the years and no one adjusted the door. The scrape marks on the floor from opening it were dug in a good quarter of an inch. We finally got in and looked around. It was CULTURE SHOCK! You had to be there to appreciate the whole of it.

The owner came out of the kitchen and Carl greeted him, "Hello, Joe!" "How's business?" Joe had a dirty looking cloth about three feet long hanging out of his front pocket. He smiled, blew his nose in the "pocket cloth" and said, "Not bad. Picking up everyday as the tourists keep moving in." Joe referred to the true "city hunters" arriving in their new, blaze-orange clothes and new boots as "Tourists." It seemed that every other guy living up there was named, Joe.

Joe, all smiles, came over to the bar, took out his long pocket cloth and wiped off the bar. I could still see a visual picture of him blowing his nose in that same "utility cloth." I also saw him wipe his hands with this when he was cooking.

We ordered, as Carl suggested, beer from a bottle. Joe was serving some of his "tourist customers" some of the "higher priced" beer. I started talking to one of the "tourist' who was sitting next to me. He had all of the brand new, blaze-orange clothes on. He told me that he rented one of the cabins from the bartender, "S" Nelson, and "put his fate" in "S"'s hands. "S" promised him the cabin, meals, drinks, and a good place to hunt. He told me that he came from Chicago to hunt up here. C-H-I-C-A-G-O .... The locals say that word slowly when someone says they are from there. "The land of milk and honey .... and ...MONEY!, in the eyes of the locals looking for "outside money" to pull them through the winter.

So far, he claimed that he didn't see any deer. "S" overheard him say that he saw no deer, so far. (That's a no no if you are the cabin owner and want to fill those cabins up.) "S" (everyone seemed to call him "S") said,

63

"Keep it down. Tomorrow, I'm going to move you to a better spot, my friend. No sense in telling everyone else."

The natives (I found out later), knew that "S" stood for "Sly". It sounded like Sly had this guy right where he wanted him. By the wallet. Sly noticeably called him "My friend" a lot. The guy looked a little meek and surely out of place with all of those brand new, blaze-orange clothes on. He stood out like someone in a Santa Claus suit compared to the locals in there.

Sly kept admiring those clothes and calling him "My friend". I was thinking, he'd be lucky if Sly didn't get some of those before the guy left.

Remember Carl did tell us that this place was different. Now, the other bartender was something else. She looked like she just came off of an all-night "toot." Her cigarette was hanging limply from the corner of her mouth. She went over to the Chicago guy and asked how the food tasted as she blew a cloud of smoke at him.

He started to cough and said that he never tasted food like this before. She looked at him a bit suspicious and not quite sure how he meant that. You should know that the Lord never did bless that bartender with anything that resembled good looks.

To tip her was more of an "Act of mercy." I noticed one guy reach out with a tip and he had his head turned the other way as he did it. One did not look at her and try to eat at the same time.

The Chicago hunter then told me that he was getting the "scoots' a lot lately and kept having "accidents" in the woods. Geno stood up on the rungs of his barstool and looked over the swinging doors into the kitchen. He said that they were just pouring more grease onto the cooking stove. "Wah!" Geno said. "I'm not hungry anymore. Those hamburgers that they're making look so greasy that if you ate one, you'd probably slide right off of your stool."

The meek Chicago guy was starting to poke at the plate of food that they served him. He looked like he didn't have the courage to put it in his mouth. He poked at it again, something like you'd poke at a downed deer that you shot to see if it was going to jump up.

We all wished him luck when we left. He probably thought with the hunting. We just hoped that he'd survive.

As we were driving back to camp and it again seemed that Dave was hitting all of the potholes, Geno said, "I really hope the little guy makes it. He probably won't see any deer with all those 'toilet breaks' he keeps taking, but he'll be a tougher man when he gets back to Chicago."

Chapter 14

A Scary Relation's Gathering
At Uncle Ed's Camp

Uncle Ed had one of the nicest camps and camp locations that I have ever seen. It was located on a scenic bend of the Big Cedar River. When you drove through the one lane, winding road leading to it, the road suddenly ran near the river on one bend. From there, a view of the camp could be seen across the river, as it stood majestically two river bends ahead.

It was a huge log cabin structure with a high, open ceiling. About 8 sets of standard size bedspring and mattresses were laid out in an upstairs loft that took up about ½ of the upstairs level. The rest was open space extending from down below, like a spacious cathedral ceiling. There was a ladder made out of cedar logs to go upstairs. A large, swing-open window upstairs near those beds would be opened at night. The small rapids from the Big Cedar River was down below and about 30 feet away. This made the night's sleep peaceful and serene. A deer would normally come and drink along the other side of the river.

When you visualize this scene, one would think, this is SURELY the place to come and relax. How could anything disturb this beautiful and peaceful scene? There were no other camps or sign of other people for at least 3-4 miles upriver and only one camp 2 miles down river.

No electricity meant no radio or TV, a traditional out-house, a nice woodpile all cut and piled for the kitchen stove and the huge wood heater. An unusual, antique, wind-up Victrola with a limited number of records was downstairs. It had a chromed, wind-up crank on its side that was an instant fascination for any kids.

There also was a sign hanging above the camp door, "God Bless This Camp." This scenario was just ripe for SOMETHING to happen. This was just too peaceful to be true. Then came our annual relations' get-together weekend. I'm sure my Uncle Ed meant well when he invited the whole relation up for this weekend.

He was always a friendly, helpful, and happy-natured guy. He knew that he had a wonderful place and always seemed to enjoy sharing it with others. Poor Uncle Ed. Either he was very forgetful or had a short memory. As a kid, I can remember that these annual "Fee-as-coos" started out well but somehow had a way of changing that would send shivers down the strongest person's back.

I remember on the ride up (we had to drive about 50 miles from our home), that my dad had been complaining, "I've got a bad feeling about this. Think about it …. locked up in a remote location with your relatives. Last year, I couldn't stop shaking until two days after we got back home." My mother would try to soothe him, and my brother and I would be smiling in the back seat wondering what things those "relative" kids would do this year?

Some years, it seemed we were lucky to survive.

We rounded the road bend close to the river and saw that Uncle Ed and his family were the first one's there. They didn't get into the camp yet, so we kids were all excited. Uncle Ed was just getting his machete out of his car's trunk. There were always some very, very, long pine snakes in there. He'd go in first to kill them and we kids would be close behind to watch the action.

He opened the door and one was crawling across the long, kitchen table. WANG! One slice and he fixed that one. Another one was winding its way upstairs by climbing one of the posts on the upstairs ladder. It was wound around there pretty good. WAP! WAP! And he had that one cut in pieces. (I never saw anything like this) one came at him from the side standing about 3 feet tall by balancing on its tail. Uncle Ed saw it, went ballistic for a second, came down on his toes and with a nice back swing, cut that one in two. Talk about action, and we were just STARTING the weekend. He then went upstairs (we were about 6 inches behind him) and threw back the covers on each bed. The fourth bed had a big pine snake all curled up between the sheets.

Not wanting to get blood on the sheets, he hit it with the flat side of the machete. It slithered out of the bed onto the floor. He pounced on it immediately and hacked it all up. That one didn't want to give up to easily. He was having a hard time backing out between the beds as we kids were almost on his back. I don't know if we wanted to get that close to the action or if we didn't want to be on the floor in case there was another one. That was the last snake that we found.

He said, "Don't say how many we found. The ladies get afraid if they think there were a lot of them." I thought, the LADIES are afraid? I could see my brother checking the seat of his pants. He was our hero with that machete. He came out of the camp first and us kids, smiling, right behind him. His wife said, "How many, Ed?" He said, "Oh, one or two." She flinched. I imagine they could hear the THUNK, THUNK, THUNK, as he was working his way through the camp.

The women seemed to have their noses wrinkled up when they went in. Then they settled down and started talking about the other relatives that hadn't arrived yet. THESE were the ones we were waiting for …. These kids were the "Holy Terrors" from wherever they came from. They didn't seem to be invited over to many strangers' homes. One thing, they were never invited over twice! Even as a kid, I thought, Uncle Ed was pretty brave inviting them to his camp. Then I remembered how I saw him swinging that machete at a bunch of hissing snakes. He seemed to like a challenge.

Just then, we could hear a car crashing through the woods coming down the road. We were all smiles. Hearing that car crash into some small Popples meant Uncle Pete was already having problems with his kids. We watched their car come closer. One headlight was just knocked out and the headlight rim was dangling from hitting the small trees. You could hear, "These are the times that try men's souls." His wife was a schoolteacher and also very religious. She was always quoting something when things went wrong.

Uncle Ed came out of the camp and threw a soup can into the river. He always took any empty cans and threw them into the river current to be carried downstream. Then he'd say, "Down to Schultz." Schultz owned the next camp down river. Each time you could watch the can floating out of sight for at least a quarter of a mile. No one thought of pollution at this time.

Uncle Pete slammed on the breaks in front of the camp. You could tell that his blood pressure was up as his face was beet red. He said to Uncle Ed, "Do you still have that machete." Uncle Ed replied, "Sure, but the snakes have been cleaned out already." "I didn't mean for the snakes," Uncle Pete snorted. "Blessed are the merciful," said his wife.

We boys smiled. This was shaping up to be a real adventure! They seemed to be off to a good start! Everyone settled in for the night. Certain things had to be done before dark, so it seemed everyone was constructively busy. The camp had a Coleman gas lantern hanging from a pulley on the high ceiling, attached with a light chain, then attached to the wall. Uncle Ed lowered the lantern and turned it off for the night.

The only light then was the moonlight coming through the upstairs window. About an hour later, Uncle Pete said, 'I think I feel something crawling in my bed." His wife said, "Go to sleep, your imagining things." (Uncle Pete DID imagine a lot of things and he was afraid of all of them.) He then said, "I think it's a snake and I'm going downstairs." Uncle Ed said, "Don't step on the floor. That's where the snakes go at night." I could see that he was smiling with his eyes shut in the moonlight.

Uncle Pete said, "I'm sleeping on top of the covers and I am not coming back here again." I could see Uncle Ed smiling and chuckling to himself.

The next morning, Uncle Pete looked like he didn't sleep all night. He always could eat a lot though, and looked forward to all of the other ladies' cooking. He was enjoying himself eating when his wife said, "Blessed are those that don't over-indulge." He looked at her blankly, like she was a bookend sitting there. Then he looked back at his plate and went right back at it.

Uncle Pete was really content after that meal and seemed to finally start to relax. In fact, he came down to the river's bank and sat there fishing with my brother and I. The mosquitoes were starting to get pesty so I went back to the camp and got the big spray gun and sprayed around where we were fishing. Uncle Pete liked that and was smiling.

Then his boy came down. Uncle Pete asked him to spray some more around him. His son, Larry, took the sprayer, sprayed Uncle Pete's back. He turned his head around, curiously, and Larry sprayed him right in the face. Accident or not, Uncle Pete jumped up and chased him into a cedar swamp. We could hear a lot of crashing around. My brother said, "I hope they don't bring back more mosquitoes from that swamp."

First Larry came out of the swamp, then Uncle Pete about 5 minutes later. My aunt, Uncle Pete's wife, always saved here son's "bacon." She appraised the situation and said, "Blessed are those that forgive." Uncle Pete said, "Hell, if I could have caught him, I'd have 'blessed' him! How can I relax up here with him working on me?"

After a while, the adults went outside to take a walk and pick wild flowers. I doubted that they would go out of eyesight of the camp and the relatives' "Children of Terror." The kids went inside the camp to explore. Now, Uncle Ed's wife had a pet cat that she adored. That cat ate as well as her husband did and probably a lot better than some of the other relatives. Larry saw the cat sleeping in the sun's rays on the camp floor. He gently picked it up and walked over to where the Coleman lantern was hooked onto the wall. He lowered the lantern and placed the cat on top of the lantern. Then raised it and the cat as high as it would go. That was an extremely high cathedral ceiling. The cat and lantern would swing by with fear in its eyes. Then the fear seemed to turn to a look like a Black Panther has when he looks at you in a circus. He wanted to jump onto someone but was afraid to let go.

Uncle Ed's boys finally stopped the action. They said they didn't want the lantern to fall down and break. That seemed reasonable? The cat ran under the stove and wouldn't come out. The adults returned in a short time. Aunty said, "That cat sure is acting odd. It doesn't want to come by anyone."

The adults started to play cards. The kids just naturally, then, went outside. Now, Larry was always picked on his younger sister, Rosey, it seemed, just for the principle of it. She did seem a little smarter than him and if he didn't TOTALLY surprise her, she could normally come out of most everything ahead of him. God seemed to give her an edge.

This time, she was picking wild flowers along the riverbank. The riverbank here was about 12 feet above the level of the river. Her back was to him and he noticed this. I watched him stalk her from about 20 feet away. All of a sudden, he charged toward her as fast as he could with his arms and hands extending in front of him. He planned on pushing her into the river.

I don't know if she saw him coming through her legs as she was bending over, but at the right second, she quickly stepped aside. He couldn't stop and ran right over the edge into open space above the river. His legs were still running, like peddling a bicycle in open space as he hit the water. KA-PLOOSH! His sister looked at him, smiled, and said, "Down to Schultz!" Mark another one up for his sister.

Larry climbed out of the river wet and more determined than ever to even things up. Later, as it was getting darker, everyone kind of drifted inside. Everything looked peaceful inside. The cat was lying in front of the warm stove, sleeping. Larry was starting to eye up the cat. I watched and figured this could be a big one. His younger sister said that she had to go to the outhouse. The adults told us kids to go outside so she wouldn't be afraid. I thought, with her mind, those ANIMALS out there better be afraid.

Larry then picked up the cat and started petting it gently and walked out with the rest of us. The cat opened its eyes, saw Larry, and didn't know if it should fight or enjoy the petting. Finally, it half-closed its eyes and seemed to relax. Rosey went to do her thing and at this time, it was really dark out.

Larry kind of waited for her behind the woodpile to pass by. He was well out of her sight. As she innocently came back along the path, I saw Larry holding the cat by the tail and "winding it up" by rotating it quickly in big circles. When she was past that woodpile by about 5 feet, he threw that now crazed cat onto her back. She GASPED! Her mouth flew open but she couldn't speak! She went into the camp walking on her tiptoes, taking small steps and it appeared like her eyeballs rolled up into their sockets.

That cat was hanging onto her back for dear life, with all four of its claws dug into her back up to its first knuckles. It looked like its eyes were rolled up into its head too! Quickly, Larry said, "Look at that! The cat must have got frightened and jumped on Rosey's back." Aunty immediately went to soothe her prized cat. She couldn't figure out why it dug its claws into her. No one jumped to soothe Rosey. Her mother said, "The Lord said that a little suffering was good for all of us." Larry listened innocently and went and sat down. His dad kind of turned his chair so his back was not directly to him.

Larry then discovered the wind-up Victrola. He wound it up, put on what seemed to be the only record and played it .... over .... and over .... again! Wind it up, and replay it.... wind it up, and replay it. The adults were again playing cards and seemed, at first, appeased by the music. I could see Uncle Pete keeping time to it with his fingers on the table. "There's a whole lot of shaking going on .... "There's a whole lot of shaking going on" .... (Over and over again!) He'd keep winding it up and "There's a whole lot of shaking going on." Then the record stuck .... "Going on .... Going on .... Going on ..." Uncle Pete threw his cards into the air and shouted, "Let me at him, let me at him! I'm supposed to

be relaxing." His wife smiled and said, "Blessed are the peacemakers," as she held him down on his chair.
Uncle Ed calmly got up and took the handle out of the machine. Larry looked at that curiously. If he knew he could have done that, he probably would have taken that nice, chromed handle out a long time ago.

As they were packing up to go back home, I heard Uncle Pete say, 'I don't want him sitting behind me." His wife said, "The other choice you have is for him to sit along side of you." I think, left on his own, Uncle Pete would have referred to put him in the trunk or let him run in front of the car. As they drove away, I noticed the sign above the door, GOD BLESS THIS CAMP, was hanging downward by one nail. Someone pulled it loose.

We kids were all smiles as they were leaving, wondering what was going to happen on the next year's annual relation-at-camp trip.

Chapter 15

Uncle Pete's Prize Pontoon Boat

There weren't many things that Uncle Pete prized in his
life. Most of his tools, fish poles, and lures, were usually
lost or broken by his son, Larry. Larry actually seemed
to ENJOY breaking things, especially if they belonged to
his Dad.

His Dad would punish him for doing something wrong
and Larry would probably then, do something like break
the tip off of one of his Dad's fish poles. His dad would
punish him again, and he would probably use his Dad's
best fishing lures and lose them.

These two just didn't ever seem to get it right. That
father and son bonding be damned. Smooth cooperation
between them would remind you of trying to push a
logging chain uphill. They seemed to be the happiest
when they didn't see each other.

Now that pontoon boat came into his life, quite by
accident. Uncle Pete always dreamed of owning a nice
boat of his own. He also dreamed of being able to go out
on the calm water and cruise along and quietly observe
Mother Nature at her best. To see the wildlife swimming
peacefully in the water relaxed him.

He loved to fish but, previously, always had to depend upon someone else taking him along in their boat to go. He was a very well-liked guy and others enjoyed taking him along….as long as he didn't bring any of his kids with. Those kids had reputations that ranged well ahead of them wherever they went.

Remember the western movies when they'd show the bad guys coming into town? The storekeepers would hurry outside and bring in their wares, pull the shades and put out the CLOSED sign? Maybe his kids didn't rate QUITE that treatment yet, but I do believe the immediate neighbors would lock their doors and pull the shades and sit in the house quietly if they were fortunate to see them coming over.

Larry was telling me, "I went over to the neighbor's the other day and their door was locked. I hollered, 'Is anyone home?' and someone inside said, 'NO'. That sure seemed strange to me."

Uncle Pete bought his 16-foot pontoon boat used, from a good friend. I think Pete's friend felt sorry for a guy that lead Pete's lifestyle and also knew his love to own his own boat. This friend was getting too old to manage the boat so he just about gave it to Uncle Pete.

The boat came with running lights, new outdoor carpeting recently installed, a nice blue canopy with an aluminum rod frame battery, a 50 horse Johnson motor, fishing rod holders, steering wheel and seat with all of the necessary controls, bench seats on three sides, anchors, and ropes.

He told me proudly that he paid $500.00 for the whole package. Looking at what he got, you could conclude that someone really liked him and just about gave it to him. Pete was all smiles. He had some of the biggest teeth that I ever have seen. A full smile kind of reminded you of a horse smiling at you. Horses are the only other thing that I ever saw that had big teeth like Pete's.

He had a plan. He made arrangements with another good friend to leave his prized pontoon boat tied up by his dock on the Menominee River. His friend was skeptical at first. He asked Pete, "You don't plan on bringing any of your kids over here, do you?" Pete had to promise him that he would not. In fact, he said, "This is the main reason that I want to store it here. I don't want my kids near it."

Uncle Pete normally had that "Hang dog" remorseful look from feeling like a loser with his bunch. Anyone with even a LITTLE compassion had to feel sorry for him. His friend agreed to let him dock it there and Pete was really happy. Somehow, he always had high blood pressure. He was looking forward to many relaxing, fishing trips on this wonderful pontoon boat.

After about two months of using his new boat, he was gaining more confidence in himself, relaxing more, and enjoying the fishing. He claimed that his blood pressure was almost back to normal. Pete even bought himself a nice cap showing that he was the boats "skipper." Nothing fancy but it had to give him a great feeling. Seeing him put that cap on and give you a smile with those huge, white teeth …. You couldn't help but think this might be as close to Heaven as he'd get. A Yooper's dream!

Uncle Pete called me up one Saturday and invited me to go for a ride on his new prized boat and do some fishing. He said, "Bring your river fishing gear. We can "still fish" or drift. I know some nice walleye holes and we'll have fun. There will be just the two of us." I could just visualize the smile on his face as he was inviting me.

I accepted and met him at his house ½ an hour later. When I got there, he was arguing with his wife. "No, No!" he said, "I promised that I'd never bring any of our kids out to Tom's. I never would have got the docking privileges there, otherwise."

She was saying, "Bring him right from the car onto your boat." Pete would reply, "No! No! She'd say, "Right from the car onto the boat. How can he hurt anything then? RIGHT FROM THE CAR ONTO THE BOAT!" Pete, the nice guy that he was, was losing this argument too. He looked at his son, Larry, and said, "Do you promise to do everything I tell you to do on the boat?" "I promise, I promise." sparkled Larry. "Do you promise to not push anything into the water?" "I promise, I promise," said Larry. "Do you promise to sit still and be quiet while we're fishing?" "I promise, I promise," smiled Larry.

Uncle Pete finally ran out of promises and told him to get into the car. His wife said that she was going too, just to sit along the river and visit with Tom's wife. Tom's wife knew my aunt and they were friends. His wife seemed to always take a lot of pills and sometimes, her head seemed to jerk to one side. This normally happened when she saw my aunt's kids. Their home on the river was supposed to be a tension reliever for her. During the week, she taught emotionally disturbed kids everyday.

We arrived at Tom's and Pete successfully got everyone on, untied his lines, and pushed off before anything could happen in Tom's yard. I noticed that Larry had a good-sized paper bag full of something that he brought with him. He placed it under his seat and seemed to forget about it.

We were off and running! Uncle Pete flashed that big, toothy smile and made a fast pass in front of Tom's property for the ladies' enjoyment. I heard his wife shout, "Be careful, Larry. I don't want you to fall in, honey." She never seemed to be concerned about Uncle Pete.

We were heading upstream to the Chappee Rapids area. Pete explained that the current from the rapids was ideal for walleye. We should catch something. We anchored in the current and began fishing. Larry never had any interest in fishing. He started to rock the boat to each side. Then he stood up and REALLY worked at it.

Uncle Pete, trying to control his blood pressure, said, "Remember all the promises you made before we started?" "You didn't say anything about rocking the boat," replied Larry. Pete gave him a look that must have been effective. The rocking stopped.

Then! Uncle Pete had a fish on! It pulled like a good-sized walleye. "Get the net," Pete shouted to Larry. Larry ran over with the net and poked it around the fish. Somehow the net and the line got tangled and the fish came off. Pete looked at Larry. Larry smiled and let the net slide into the river. Pete lurched for it and missed. Luckily, I was sitting further back and caught it as it drifted by.

Uncle Pete's face was now turning red. He said, "I'm taking you back." So we reeled in and pulled the anchor. Pete sat in the Captain's seat behind the steering wheel, was breathing heavily, and going almost full-speed back to the dock. He stared straight ahead.

I should tell you, Pete feared two things in life, bats and pine snakes. Larry, of course, knew this. He sat well behind Pete and picked up his huge, paper bag that he had brought along. For the first time, I noticed, the bag was moving! Something alive was in there!

Uncle Pete continued to stare straight ahead, giving it more throttle to get in faster. Larry, sitting behind him, opened his bag and a 5-foot pine snake came slithering out. Larry took his fish pole and was nudging it to climb up onto the Captain's chair.

Then he said to his Dad, "Look below you. A pine snake just swam onto the boat." Uncle Pete saw it climbing up the chair's leg and jumped onto the seat with his feet. The snake crawled higher onto the aluminum roof framework. The snake reached the top of the seat, hissed, and coiled into circles and settled in.

Uncle Pete's eyes were now open so wide that they looked bigger than his teeth. We zoomed past Tom's shoreline and I don't think Pete even knew how to stop. He was hanging onto that roof for all he was worth and steering yet, with his feet.

Pete's wife saw us go by at such a high rate of speed and said, "Look at that. Pete is showing off for us ladies. Did you ever see anyone else steer a boat like that?" Pete was now going, 'YAAA HOO HOO! YAAA HOO

HOO!" Tom's wife jumped up and said, "That man's in trouble!" Pete's wife then said, "No, he always sounds that way when he and his son get together." Tom's wife took another look and went into the house for a hand-full of pills. SHE KNEW!!

Larry was still nudging the snake with his fish pole and Uncle Pete was swinging a boat gaff pole that he had wedged under the roof supports at Larry. I didn't like pine snakes either but felt that I better do something soon. We were now running wide open (Uncle Pete had one of his feet on the throttle), and the steering didn't seem to be under control.

I hooked a paddle under the snake and threw it overboard. Then, I pulled back on the throttle and helped Uncle Pete down from the roof. He came down but couldn't get one hand free. He had a death grip on the roof.

His face was now beet red. One could only guess what his blood pressure was. It took him a while to get words to come. His mouth was working but there was no sound. He looked at his son, Larry, who was smiling back at him. Larry said, "Look, your cap is floating down river. It must have fell in." Uncle Pete looked like he had a tear in his eye as he watched that cap disappear. I patted him on the back and said, "Take it easy. It could have been the boat."

Pete eased the boat in and tied it up. Everyone on the shore was watching. His friend, Tom, stayed in the house and watched through the window. His wife was swallowing a few new pills …. SHE KNEW! Uncle Pete's wife said, "If you weren't showing off with steering with your feet, you probably would still have yor cap."

Larry made a dash for the car. His wife said, "So, you plan on leaving all of your fishing stuff on the boat this time?" Pete just looked straight ahead and walked to the car. We all got into the car, Uncle Pete reached up to pull down his cap visor that wasn't there, put the car in gear and we started home.

I looked behind and saw his friend, Tom and his wife, standing in the middle of the road watching us go ....

Chapter 16

Crazy Jack and The Bear Cubs

Jack was something else. Everyone that knew him called him "Crazy Jack." You never knew what he was going to do next. He had a good sense of humor and if you weren't the subject of his joke, he was fun to be around.

My camp is blessed with some real different visitors. They are all from the U.P. or near area. Some have moved farther away because of their jobs. They always come back when they can and love to tell stories of some adventures that they created?

Most would act on an impulse in the wild and read the rules about it later. They are the types that if you had to go to war, you'd appreciate having them alongside of you. Honest, sincere and they wouldn't let you down.

Crazy Jack is one like that. His eyes sparkled and he had a smile from ear to ear. Jack worked at a paper mill during the week. He was a relatively quiet guy at work and loved his freedom on the weekends. Most weekends he'd hunt or fish.

Bill said, "Hey, Jack. Tell the guys about how you caught the bear cubs and don't leave anything out." Tim was starting to twist uncomfortably on his chair. He's normally Jack's hunting and fishing partner. There was a few embarrassing times in this story that he hoped Jack might overlook. Not Crazy Jack! He made a point to tell ALL of the story. After all, this is what gave it the flavor.

"Well," Jack started, "Tim and I were going up to the Pemene Falls area (on the Menominee River). We were taking my boat and Tim's motor. First we had to have night crawlers, so we went to the Menominee cemetery the night before. They run the sprinklers almost all day, so the crawlers were easy to find in the dark with your flashlight. Tim went one way and I went another. We figured that we'd circle and come back together with plenty of crawlers." Tim started to clear his throat and shuffle his feet as he sat listening by the camp's kitchen table.

"Well, guys, you know that Tim has always been my outdoors partner. I never saw him show any fear under pressure. I was thinking about that now. Here we were. Alone in the pitch black night in the cemetery among all the dead folk."

"Then I spotted a new grave just dug. It was right in line where Tim was coming. He didn't see it because he had his flashlight shining about 2 feet ahead of him, looking intently, for a night crawler. I figured that I'd test his courage. I slid down into that open grave hole without him seeing me. Finally he came within a foot of it and was looking the other way. I reached out and grabbed him by the ankle. He threw his flashlight over his head and let out a scream that could have awakened the dead. At the same time, he jumped up into the air and almost pulled me right out of that hole, too."

Tim smiled and said, "I promised the Lord a lot of things in those few seconds before I shook loose and ran away from there." Crazy Jack said, "I still figure that Tim is brave, …. Just that he probably is afraid of ghosts." Tim looked at him and just shook his head.

"Tell them about the time that the motor came off of the boat, Jack." Jack adjusted his cap visor, "We'll save that for another time." It didn't sound like he was anxious to tell that one to us.

"Having our bait, we then drove up to the Nathan area the next day. Driving in the last one-lane road, Tim spotted two bear cubs up in a tree. The tree was alongside a small field just off of the road. They appeared to be small, harmless cubs. I told Tim to drive near the tree and I'd climb it and we'd catch the cubs. (Crazy Jack had no idea what he would do with two bear cubs.) Well, guys, I looked around for a while and we didn't see any mother bear. I then climbed that tree. About ¾ of the way up, the first cub was hanging onto a side limb. He looked like a little Teddy bear, so, I reached out for him. He swung his arm and claws at me so fast that I didn't see it coming. He caught me across the side of my face and down one arm. My shirtsleeve was torn in shreds and I started to feel warm blood on my face and arm."

"When I jerked back, Tim hollered up," "He just got in a lucky one. Go after him." Crazy Jack said, "I couldn't quit now. He was too small to be afraid of. I reached for him again and he let out a wail that you probably could hear a 40 away." Tim said, "This was the time to worry. I was down on the ground where the mother bear probably was. Jack was safe up in the tree."

Jack said to Tim, "I should be able to catch him by the back of the neck and drop him down to you. Get a jacket from the truck, hold it out and I'll drop it right in the jacket." Tim went and got (to play it safe) Jack's jacket. He stood under the tree with the jacket opened wide.

Jack looked down, saw Tim below, and grabbed the bear cub by the nape of the neck and jerked it free from the limb. That cub came toward him like a "buzz-saw." Its claws were swatting at whatever it could touch. It swung right into Jack.

Crazy Jack shouted out in pain but didn't let go. His shirt was now torn into ribbons and looked like it was bleeding. He finally pulled it free from himself. Its claws were digging everywhere. Jack's arms and nose got the worst of this. He finally dropped it down. Tim said, "I'll say this for him. He dropped it right into the jacket. I covered it quickly with the rest of the jacket and it felt like I was holding onto a hornet's nest after someone kicked it."

"I just got it inside the pick-up and looked up at Jack. He had the other cub by the neck. It wouldn't let go of the limb but was wailing like crazy. The mother bear must have heard the commotion as I suddenly heard something crashing through the woods toward us. I jumped into the truck and locked the doors. That mother bear then stood up hanging onto the front truck fender and was looking through the windshield. She looked 9 feet tall!"

"I told Jack that I did what I thought he'd do. I started the motor and drove away! I figured that I'd distract the mother bear from him and the tree. Jack didn't look convinced …..He said after I left him, that little cub was screaming for all it was worth. The mother bear (all 9 feet of her) came and stood under the tree and looked up at him."

Jack said that he smiled at the cub, tried to pet it to quiet it down but all it did was keep on whimpering. The mother bear now was directly under the tree. She stood up and was bouncing the trunk of the tree with one paw and then would hit it hard with the other. It seemed to be trying to decide if it could climb that small tree.

Jack explained, "Every time that big bear hit the tree trunk, I'd feel it all the way up to where I was. I looked down at that big mother, talked softly to her, tried to sing to her, and smiled nice at her. Boys, I'm here to tell you, a big mother bear won't smile back at you. I looked at that cub and I do believe that IT was smiling back at me. It knew I was in a fix."

Then Tim came back with the pick-up, blowing the horn to get that mother bear's attention and let the first cub go free. The mother walked over by the first cub smelled it, looked at Tim in the truck suspiciously, and walked off out of sight with cub number one.

Everyone asked how he got down safely. "I stayed in that tree until my legs got numb. Then my brave partner, Tim, backed the truck up within 20 feet from the tree. I climbed down and stiff-legged, swung my legs until I got in to the truck. My jacket was all ripped up." Tim said, "We were lucky. If it wasn't for your jacket, that bear could have wrecked the inside of the truck." Somehow, that didn't seem to make Jack any happier.

"I asked Crazy Jack if he still wanted to go fishing. He just looked straight ahead and said, 'Just drive!', laughed Tim.

Chapter 17

The Time We Lost the Boat

There were three of us going on this well-planned fishing trip. Toby, his younger brother Frightened Frank, and myself. Toby said that his mother must have been frightened by a thunderstorm, dreamed of snakes, and water when Frank was born, as these were his greatest fears.

Toby had his own 13-foot, plywood boat. Most boats were either 12-feet or 14-feet but Toby's was, for some reason, 13-feet long. This made it a bit small for 3 people. It was made out of ¼ inch outdoor plywood and I'll say this, it was very strongly built.

His trailer was not a real boat trailer. It was a two-wheeled utility (it hauled everything) trailer with a one-foot high boxed frame on top. The frame had hinges on the front end as well as the back end, like hinged tailgates.

When he hauled his boat, he would unhinge the front and back so the boat rested on the trailer's floor with the boat sticking over the front and back of the trailer. We'd tie it down with ropes to the trailer. The trailer was attached to the car with a standard ball hitch but NO SAFETY CHAINS! Oh, Toby had chains all right, but he would always just lay them over the hitch for looks only. I guess he didn't believe much in them.

We loaded all of our gear the night before, as Toby said we'd start early the next day. We'd eat at "Greasy Gene's" bar and grill. He explained, "Gene never shuts off that grill."

Carl, a north woods friend of Toby's, was going to meet us by L'Anse. We were going to fish the Huron River for trout. Carl was to be our guide and cook. Toby told us, "Carl has his own boat so all we have to do is follow him." We drove north again for about two hours and Toby smiled, "We're here, at Greasy Gene's place. Time to eat!"

"If the breakfast is too greasy," muttered Toby, "Ask for more bread. Bread will soak it up in your stomach." Armed with this good knowledge, we got out of the car and started in. There was a lot of deep grass close to the building and door. Frightened Frank looked sideways constantly, like, he expected a pine snake to leap out at any time.

"Greasy Gene" was all smiles when we came in. He was really friendly to Toby. I guessed that he didn't see too many repeat customers. He looked like any north woods native that you'd expect to see, except for his apron. It had most every color on it that went with food. Red Ketchup, yellow Mustard, red meat, some green stuff and brown ..... Lots and lots of brown. Some of it was old and some was new.

We all ordered hamburgers and coffee. Toby leaned over and whispered, "He don't wash his hands, but remember

that grill has to be hot to cook so it also kills the germs."
Everyone ate and no one smiled.

Toby knew of a two-lane County road with less traffic, so
we turned onto it and were again going north. We finally
arrived at L'Anse. There was Carl, sleeping against a
tree where he said he would be. After meeting everyone,
he quickly told us the "game plan" and seemed really
anxious to go fishing. He said, "I've got my boat hidden
alongside the river so I don't have to tow it. It MAY
hold two of us. I don't know, because I normally fish
alone."

He had the appearance of a natural woodsman. If he
wanted to, he could probably guide you to some very
good fishing spots. His clothes may have been called
"Earth tone" but they were actually all faded out. He
could stand in the woods and you probably wouldn't
notice that he was even there.

"If you fellas brought the bread, drinks, and potatoes,
I've got the spices, cooking oil, and frying pan. I'll cook
and I think that you'll like it." He looked about as dirty,
all over, as Greasy Gene's apron. He said, "Living by
yourself in the woods doesn't give you the chance to do
the washing too often." We all just smiled back at him. I
figured that you would never lose this guy in the woods
at night. If he came close enough, you could smell him.
He probably knew all of the trout "fishing holes" though.

Carl led off with his old pick-up truck. He said, "It
smokes a lot but still goes where I want to go." We had
to drive a good distance behind him, as his smoke was
worse than the road dust. Finally, he slowed down to a
crawl and pointed down to the left of us. The river was

bubbling near the road here. With all of the grown up ferns and trees, you never would have seen it if you didn't know the way there.

We stopped and turned into what appeared to be an old, grown-over, logger's landing (a small area bulldozed flat to pile logs in). The brush and grass was grown about "belly high" across it. Carl turned in there and made a U-turn to park. He said that he knew where the holes were so he was dodging them. Being that we didn't, we parked just behind him. "You boys carry your boat and things down to the river. I'll walk ahead and scout for my boat. I haven't been down here for a while."

We easily pulled the boat down and were just happy to be out walking again. "Here it is," shouted Carl. We caught up with him and low and behold, his boat was one big sized Mortar box! It was one sheet of solid tin except for a wooden board on the two up-turned ends. Carl was all smiles, and said, "I caught a lot of fish out of this baby. It doesn't take much water to float it."

The river was anywhere from one foot deep along the shore to 10-12 feet deep in the holes. "Why don't one of you fish with him and we'll have two in each boat?" Carl said. Now, Frightened Frank was the first in line and closest to Carl's "Boat." I said, "Go ahead, Frank. It looks like a lot of room in there." Carl was already seated and holding onto the boat and some tree limbs to steady it. The seats were two loose boards reaching across from one side to the other.

Frank looked at the boat in disbelief. He never saw anyone fish out of anything like this. Come to think of it, either did I. Frightened Frank was nervous, but he held onto a tree limb, put one foot in and sat down kind of hard on the seat. That Mortar-box boat immediately sank to the bottom. Although the water was only 2 feet deep, Frank jumped out dripping wet, in a panic. He said, "I knew something like this was going to happen. I just knew it!" Carl said, "Sometimes she floats …. and sometimes she don't" Frank looked at him in terror….

We then had 3 in our boat and Carl in the lead with his boat. When that mortar box floated over a trout hole, those fish must have thought night had come quickly.

The mosquitoes and fish were biting about equally well, except, the mosquitoes never missed. After we sat on those boat seats for two hours, that meal from Greasy Gene's was noticeably starting to work on everyone. Carl noticed us sliding around uncomfortably on our seats and said, "We'll go up to the next steep river bank and make a meal. You can take a toilet break and I'll cook. Geeze, watching you guys squirm on your seats, you'd think that you ate at Greasy Gene's."

That was a welcome toilet break for all of us, and I'll tell you, the Game Law Digest does not make good toilet paper.

We had a total of 12 trout and decided to fry them all up. Carl was a typical backwoods cook. He never washed his hands. He unfolded the handle of his frying pan, put in the grease that he had in a pint jar, a little Cajun seasoning mix that he claimed he blended himself. I figured that the Cajun mix would well, offset any unclean flavor. Toby and I watched him cook, with interest, and Frightened Frank seemed to watch with suspicion. The meal was good. We ate everything. Cooking over an open wood fire makes all of the utilities turn black from the smoke. The bean can was jet black but the beans inside were good.

It was now getting darker in the woods. "Let's start back while we still have any daylight," said Toby. So we rowed back upstream, got the boat back onto the trailer and tied it down extra strong. We felt that it wouldn't come off no matter what speed we went.

Toby, never connecting the safety chains, looped them over the trailer hitch so they looked convincing. We started back at a good rate of speed. Toby would have one of us, by habit, look back about every 10-20 minutes to see that there were no trailer problems.

We were traveling this two-lane, pot-holed, county road of many curves. Every ½ mile seemed to have a sweeping curve. Looking back, all was O.K. Then, Toby said, "Check the trailer again." There was a long silence. "What's the matter?" said Toby. Frank said, "There's no boat OR trailer back there." He eased it to a stop and turned around. We checked back as far as the last time that we saw it but still saw no sign of the boat or trailer.

The roadsides along here were all woods and no houses. There were no houses in sight. Toby said, "It just couldn't disappear. We'll go slower and check again." On one tight curve, we saw two tire tracks going through the sand ditch and disappear at the wood's edge. There was a solid stand of 1-2 inch Popple trees along the woods that appeared perfectly normal.

We knew that those tracks had to go SOMEWHERE. We walked in line with those tire marks made in the ditch. About 50 yards through the Popples and ON SOMEONE'S BACK LAWN, stood our trailer and boat, unharmed.

There was a guy standing up by a lawn chair looking at it like a space ship had landed. He said, "I was sitting here quietly and suddenly that trailer and boat came crashing out of the woods and stopped 20 feet from me! The trailer tongue was standing straight out until it stopped." He was rightfully upset. He was even getting Frightened Frank upset.

Toby, always the fast thinker, went and got the car, said, "Yeah, Yeah. Strange things can happen." He hooked it back up while the landowner was still in shock, thanked him, and we drove away.

We thought about it and figured that the boat front, shaped like a wedge, and the high speed of the trailer, knifed its way over those 14 foot high Popples. They must have bent over and sprung back up again so quickly that they didn't show noticeable signs of even bending.

"Now, I can see the need for safety chains," Toby said. "I'm going to fix some up that work." I said, "Frightened Frank is talking to himself and staring again .... something about never going fishing with us again."

"Fright tends to make a person say odd things," countered Toby, "I don't know why Frank is always so afraid ....

Chapter 18

Deer Tales From the U.P. Rabbit's Camp (This Last Season – Cousin Tim's Version)

It's the second week of deer camp (Monday) and I'm writing this from our camp on the back of some old calendar pages. All in all, we did pretty well. Bill saw a 14 pointer the first morning. He shot at it, all running shots, with his lever action .300 Savage. He shot, rapid fire, 3 times, and 2 "clicks" later, he was out of shells. He thought that he put 5 shells in his gun. He looked on the ground and there were 3 empty shells and 2 full ones. "I don't know how they got there," he said, "but I was working that lever pretty fast."

His son, Tim, who was in a close blind, said, "I 'hit the dirt' and hugged it until Bill stopped shooting." Bill's wife, who was in the camp, said, "It sounded like a machine gun the way he was shooting." Tim said later, that he felt fortunate that Bill ran out of shells. The buck ran away with only minor wounds.

Vic, who hunted for the first two days, said, "There's sure not many deer here." He hunted in a nice blind about 35 yards from the camp's door. He left for home on Friday morning at 7:30 AM. Bob then sat in that blind. At 9:00 AM, a nice spikehorn buck came walking through. He handled that with a heart shot. He said, "That sure was easy compared to missing that 8 pointer on opening day." A standing shot through some brush. Bob said, "I like to think that the brush deflected the bullet." (No one ever wants to admit to a miss.)

Bill redeemed himself and shot a spikehorn on opening day. Rev. Tim, dropped a spikehorn on the second day, and on the third day, Bob got a spikehorn.

The morning before season, the talk seemed to be all about the miracle of buck lures. Tim had a new one, "Wilderness Passion?" He claims that was what brought in the 14 pointer to Bill. The guys were talking about which one was the best. Names like, "Dangerous Mood", "Irresistible", "Acorn Madness", and "One Jump" were a few of the highly recommended.

Vic, who is rarely ever outdone by someone else's story, said, "Those are nothing, guys. Compared to a lure that I used a few years ago. I put some of it on the tips of both of my hunting boots and walked about 500 yards to my tree blind during bow season. I started up the ladder and looked below me. About 15 yards behind, was a huge 10 point buck following my tracks."

Bob said, "If it worked that good, we should put some on your boots again and let you walked through the cedar swamp and back. You might be like the Pied Piper and lead all of the deer back to us." Vic didn't say "squat" after that. He just started to smile and shake up the wood stove's fire.

We all saw a good share of does and still have a "8 point or better" tag to fill and a few doe tags. We could have used my number one son, Randy, in a key blind in back of the 40. We saw a nice 8 pointer walked past it at

11:00 AM on the first day. No one was close enough for a good shot. Randy just mustered out of a lengthy career in the Army. Adjustment back into normal civilian life can be somewhat difficult for some. We hope to have him with us for next year's season. He's an excellent shot and an "elected" deer dragger.

It's snowing out right now at camp. Everyone went home Friday night and I'm the first one back (Sunday night). The back yard is criss-crossed with fresh deer tracks. We had scattered some loose corn out there before we left on Friday.

I see headlights coming in. Tim just pulled in from Engadine. He said, "There's a foot of snow up that way right now." We have about 3-4 inches here, in Lake Township. He's got a big smile. He just loves the camp life. The wood fire crackling, checking for deer in the back yard, and attempting to out-tell deer stories like us older members. Father Tim blessed and gave out St. Hubert metals to the deer hunters at his masses this past weekend. He and his Dad also had one. I had to rough it. That could explain why mine was a more difficult shot than their's was.

We told him about the three bear that we saw by his deer blind. I'm not sure he believed us but as Bill says, "I never see him falling asleep in that blind anymore." TV 6 (Marquette) just put a news strip across the screen. "More snow and slippery roads coming." We don't mind. We're already here and seem to have enough food for another month. My wife made our Thanksgiving meal this past Sunday rather than next Thursday. She's a nurse and works on Thanksgiving Day. She's a wonderful cook and makes all of the traditional "fixings" with a big turkey.

After two huge helpings, my stomach feels like I swallowed a rock. She makes the best homemade stuffing that I have ever tasted. I've got a lot of the leftovers up here at camp. We'll be sitting in pretty good shape for eating.

There wasn't a lot of gunshots fired in our "listening" area, so it would appear that the deer-kill was somewhat down in the area. The camps that we visited seemed to have done "medium-well." Not many camps filled all of their buck tags yet, although there still is time left to hunt.

(Tuesday), The David Peterson camp members came over to check how we did. It's 10:30 AM. They normally fill with nice bucks but didn't see a horn for the whole first week. It's unusual. We never see each other for the entire year except at deer camp, where we are the best of friends.

We took them over to see our "Buck Hanging Post." We have a nice rack from a 10 point buck that we skillfully wired onto the head of a doe or smaller buck. Hanging so high on the "post," it looks like the real thing. After the visitors get over the shock of seeing such a nice rack on a much smaller deer, we all get a good laugh. They then want to know where and when we shot that huge 10 pointer.

The excitement of hunting the deer is a strong point, although, the annual camp life with the new stories, good-natured joking, being in the woods early in the morning, watching the sun rise up over the trees, being frightened by an "exploding" partridge flying up in front of you while walking to your post in the dark, hearing the late-arriving geese flying high overhead, and trying your darnest to stay awake in that early morning cold is all part of the "Hunt Experience." These are all of the memories that we daydream about until the next season.

Chapter 19

Shaky Sam and the Seagull Omen

I was sitting out in a lawn chair peacefully in my yard one day last month. The day was beautiful. I was thinking, what could ever go wrong today?

Within 5 minutes, Sam drove up and stopped to visit. I saw him coming and started to tense up. Any trips or adventures with him could prove dangerous to your health. He had that look in his eye like he was planning something.

He jumped out of his car and said, "Have I got a fishing trip planned for us! Big trout. REALLY BIG! A salesman came in this last week and told me all about it. I believe him because he went into a lot of details."

I looked up at him and just then a seagull flew over and dropped a big white splotch right on my shoulder. That should have been an omen. Someone else was trying to tell me something. Sam glanced at that and it didn't even phase him. He was used to bigger stuff than that. He started to talk about the fishing trip again.

Sam was a high school principal. He often said that his job was like a war except no one ever completely wins. This year, a student threw a 3-inch firecracker under his desk when he was quietly working. Another time, someone put a pine snake in his top desk drawer. When he reached into that drawer for a pencil and grabbed the snake, they said that he yanked it out of the desk as he jumped up and he and his secretary looked like cross-country track racers as they ran down the hall.

Another time, the kids took his wooden steps going up to his mobile home door and burned them at a football bonfire. He said that God was with him as he left the house in the dark. He was still hanging on to the doorknob when he dropped from the missing steps.

Once again, these "creative" high school kids knew that he parked his car very close to the school building in the only "natural" parking spot available there. This time, they rang a false alarm. The fire trucks came. The fire chief immediately saw this car so close to the building that he announced to move it further away, immediately!

Sam ran out, thinking it was the real thing started his car, put it in gear and all it would do was roar! The kids had jacked it up on blocks just enough off of the ground that the wheels didn't touch and all the tires would do was spin.

By this time of the year, his nerves were frazzled and his blood pressure was pumping on high. The poor guy really needed to get away. He didn't get that nickname, Shaky Sam, for nothing. The fishing solitude always seemed to help relax him. But now there was another problem. At this time of the year, he was beyond normal from his job. He no longer took natural precautions on these trips and could be down right dangerous.

Smiling and with his hands slightly shaking, he said, "This is on the Au Train Bay and the Au Train River. We can rent a boat and motor up there and not worry about the normal problems of pulling a boat that far." I can remember one time when his boat trailer came free from the trailer hitch on the highway. We were lucky that no one got killed.

I couldn't think of a good reason why I couldn't go with him but yet was hesitating on an answer. That seagull was starting to circle overhead again. If it dropped another one on me, that would have helped with the decision.

We agreed to go the following week. Sam came early, Monday, with his new pick-up truck. I'll say this for principals; they can afford a few extras if they can survive their job. Sam was all smiles and said, "What a way to relax after having a year like I had."

We drove up to the "Misty Dunes" cabins and boat rentals. Sam had a good map from his salesman friend. The owner was skeptical about renting us a boat, trailer, and motor to take away from his place. He normally rented the equipment to be used right there. Sam did some "name dropping" of his friend who went there regularly and highly recommended them to us. It seemed to appease the boat owner. We got the boat set up and we were on our way. Sam might have been developing a nervous twitch from the job, but he was really good with the public relations end of it.

We finally arrived up into the fishing area where Sam wanted to fish. We unloaded the boat, loaded our equipment in, and were ready. Now I started to get nervous. Sam was normally, "Hell on Wheels" with any rental equipment. He seemed to feel that way he was "getting his money's worth." He usually had the reputation of tipping over the boat once on a weeklong fishing trip. So far, he never did this with me. I couldn't figure out how he'd do this, as I never tipped over a boat by accident in my life.

Sam started the motor and I noticed there was no stream of water coming out of that little hole in the motor where its supposed to. He was idling it in the sand and it was sucking sand into the water pump. We fixed that quickly. Trolling for trout in the Au Train Bay gave us 3 trout. Then the sky started to cloud up quickly. The wind came up and the bay immediately started to make "white caps." Sam eased us over to a sheltered shore somewhere near, he said, William's Island.

There was a shallow stream on one side where he said that we should go to "say out of the rough stuff." The waves were now about 3 feet high but this stream was shallow. Remember at this time of the year, Sam seemed not to fear anything! Those kids really did a job on conditioning him. "We've got to cross some of that open water area to get up that stream," shouted Sam. The current was blowing us crossways to the waves. I never believed that anyone would intentionally drive a boat crossways to the waves. Sam did.

The front of the boat was way out of the water and swinging dangerously about 2 feet to the right and to the left. Water was splashing over our bodies and getting us drenched. I was sitting in the middle seat and clawed my way along the boat's bottom to reach the front seat and hold it down. NOW, I could see how he tipped those boats over. After getting both of us good and wet and the boat ½ full of water, we reached the mouth of that stream. He ran us full-throttle up that shallow stream. The water here wasn't deep enough for a motor, let alone, at full speed.

The propeller was bouncing and scrapping between rocks steady. I looked over and could have sworn that I saw sparks from the prop, hitting the rocks. Sam was all smiles and said, "We made it!" (In a tone of voice that he surprised himself.) He had no mercy on rental equipment. We had 4 nice fish at this time.

Sam's eyes seemed glazed over and he said, "Should we try it out there again?" I didn't know if he had a death wish or was really that dedicated of a fisherman. If he'd have tried it, I figured that I could have stunned him with an oar to the head and keep us beached.

That new boat now had rock dents all along its bottom and the propeller had to have pieces missing from roaring through the rocks. We returned the boat and motor to the rental guy. He looked at it like he didn't recognize it.

Sam said to him, "You've got a nice boat and motor. I'll probably come back soon, again." The guy just looked at his equipment …. Then at Sam …. and kept shaking his head from side to side.

I thought, "If God ever gives me a sign again, like that seagull, I promise to follow it."

BOB HRUSKA'S OTHER BOOKS AVAILABLE:

*HUMOROUS STORIES FROM THE U. P. HUNTING CAMPS &
HUMOROUS FISHING STORIES FROM THE U.P.*

If You Like Patrick McManus,
You Will Love Bob Hruska's

THE HUMOROUS HUNTING BOOK = 30 stories that took place mostly in Menominee County, through manly deer, rabbit, and bird hunters who read this book will be reminded of similar incidents that took place at their own camps. There is a cast of characters that no respectful collection of hunting tales could be without.

THE HUMROUS FISHING BOOK = These 23 stories turn some scary adventures into hilarity. They include some fly-in trout fishing trips to Canada, as well as fishing trips closer to home in the U.P. The stories are guaranteed to keep you smiling from page 1 on.

SEND FOR AN AUTOGRAPHED COPY. Excellent Reading or Gift!!

QUANTITY   COST

_____   HUMOROUS STORIES FROM   _____
                     THE U.P. HUNTING CAMPS
                     ($10.00 Postage Pd)

_____   HUMOROUS FISHING STORIES   _____
                     FROM THE U.P.
                     ($10.00 Postage Pd)
                                        TOTAL   _____

NAME_____
ADDRESS_____
CITY_____STATE_____
ZIP_____
Make checks payable to: Robert R. Hruska
140 S. Birch Ave., Gillett, WI 54124